Shaq # 32
Sned

SHAQ ATTAQ!

SHAQUILLE O'NEAL

with Jack McCallum

SHAQ ATTAQ!

 HYPERION New York

ISBN: 1-56282-720-0
First Edition
10 9 8 7 6 5 4 3 2 1

This book is dedicated to my parents,
Philip and Lucille Harrison,
and my grandmothers,
Cillar O'Neal,
Irma Harrison,
and Odessa Chambliss.

ACKNOWLEDGMENTS

The authors would also like to gratefully acknowledge the assistance of Leonard Armato and Dennis Tracey, Shaquille's agent and personal assistant respectively.

CONTENTS

SHAQ ATTAQ!

CHAPTER ONE

Who's That Knockin' at My Door?

By January, two months into my professional basketball career, a lot of crazy things had happened to me. I had signed the largest rookie contract in the history of sports—$41 million for seven years. I had become Reebok's main spokesman, and my commercials, with basketball greats like Wilt Chamberlain, Bill Russell, Kareem Abdul-Jabbar, and Bill Walton, were about to get some serious air time. I'd been the NBA's first player of the week and also rookie of the month two straight times. I was leading all centers in the fan voting for the All-Star game. I had rapped on Arsenio, dunked on Patrick Ewing and a lot of other big-time players, talked coast-to-coast on ESPN, signed about a million autographs, met Muhammad Ali, played pickup ball with Magic Johnson, even turned down an offer from a guy who wanted to bottle my sweat and sell it as perfume. That's a lot of action for a big kid who used to have two left feet.

But you know what sticks out? January 11, 1993, the day that the great Michael Jordan came looking for me.

Our game against Chicago was scheduled for the next night, the twelfth, but the Bulls had come to Orlando two days early, mostly so Michael could play golf. And one of his favorite courses in Florida is the one I happen to live on, Isleworth. Arnold Palmer plays there, too, and Lou Holtz, the Notre Dame coach, owns the lot next door. As far as golf goes, I tend to agree with Karl Malone who calls it "a waste of pasture-land." (As you'll see, that's about the only thing I agree with Karl Malone on.) Someone gave me a personalized set of clubs when I moved into the development and so far they've served me pretty well. They look nice standing there in the corner of my rec room, and, once in a while, when I have to make a difficult pool shot from the corner and I'm running out of space, I can pull out the putter and use the top end of it. It's shorter than my cue stick.

Jordan had played the day before at Interlachen Country Club in Orlando, but when the news got out he was mobbed at the eighteenth hole and had to hang around and sign over three hundred autographs. But Isleworth has excellent security, which is one of the reasons I bought a house there. Michael was playing with Ricky Jackson, a linebacker for the New Orleans Saints who I've known since my college days at LSU. I wasn't around when Michael knocked at my door, but he left a message with Dennis Tracey, my roommate. And when I got home I wandered out on the course and found him and Ricky out on the tenth hole. We didn't talk very long because I'm not the type of person to bother someone with idle chitchat. Ricky said he needed some tickets and I told him I'd hook him up. Michael said he'd see me tomorrow night. I said I'd be there.

Something similar had happened during my last year at

LSU when there was a knock at my apartment door early one morning. I got up, rubbed the sleep out of my eyes, and there stood Julius Erving, my childhood idol, the guy who was really the first Michael Jordan, the first guy who seemed to defy gravity out on the basketball court. The Doctor had heard about me and stopped down for a visit, which really left me in awe.

It wasn't quite the same thing with Jordan. I was older by this time—okay, only a year older but still older—and I was a professional, playing in the same league with Michael. But it was still special. Because sooner or later, everything—all the money, all the endorsements, all the publicity—came down to playing. And I was going to be playing against Michael Jordan. The game is always about putting it on the line against the great ones, and he's the greatest.

Now, I didn't look at the game as a one-on-one showdown type of thing. By that time, all the talk about Shaq versus Patrick Ewing, Shaq versus David Robinson, Shaq versus Hakeem Olajuwon, Shaq versus Alonzo Mourning, Shaq versus Wilt Chamberlain, who retired when I was one year old, had gotten silly. Basketball, at least to my way of thinking, isn't about one individual playing against another individual. That's what happens in video games.

And it's not that I wanted to "Be like Mike," either. Nothing even close to that. Part of the reason I signed with Reebok is that I wanted to be number one there instead of just another guy at Nike, where Michael is the king. I'm an individual, my own person, and I believe you get yourself in a lot of trouble if you try to copy somebody else's style. I don't act like Michael Jordan and I don't shave my head because Michael Jordan does. (I shave it because I really don't have time to take care of it. And because it makes me look a little intimidating.) There's only one Michael Jordan, just like there's only one Shaquille O'Neal.

But I knew my first meeting with Michael on the court would be special.

5

That's because Jordan is special. First of all, he's a great player. And he works hard, despite his natural talents. I know something about that because all my life I've heard that I'm only good because I'm big. You know what I'd be if I was six feet tall, instead of seven feet tall? I'd be a six-foot superstar because I would've worked at it. I guarantee you, bro, when you've gotten to Jordan's level, it's because you dropped a thousand gallons of sweat along the trail.

Also, Jordan's got personality on the court. He's good for the game. I don't care much for players who stand out there with stone faces, never reacting to anything. I know I wouldn't pay my money to see them. Fans like to see flesh-and-blood players who smile and get a little nasty once in a while. Jordan doesn't talk a lot of trash, but when he does, he backs it up. Guys like that can talk all they want. Players like Jordan, Julius Erving, and Magic Johnson made the NBA what it is today, and I'd like to continue what they've done.

Jordan's got kind of a superhero part to his game, too. He does things other players just can't do, and he makes it all look easy. Think about this for a minute. About ten times a game Jordan goes up on one side of the basket, takes some impossible twisting shot, makes it, and comes down on the other side of the basket. Maybe everybody in the NBA can make that play once in a while, but Jordan does it any time he wants. There's nobody like that.

But what I like most about Michael is the way he's handled his fame. By the time we met up in January I had an idea of what his life was like and how crazy it is, and I can tell you, bro, it's not easy being a public figure.

I like the image Michael's made for himself, an image of a good guy who gets involved in the community, likes kids, has a lot of self-confidence but isn't just some crazy egomaniac. I remember thinking, back when I was at LSU, that the great thing about Jordan was that he got cheered in every arena around the NBA, and how I'd like to be that kind of player. Well, maybe he doesn't get cheered in Detroit and Cleveland, because he's stuck it to them so many times, but that's their loss, not his.

But, see, being a good person and a great player isn't enough for some people. It seemed like the whole country went crazy during the 1993 playoffs when they found out Jordan went to Atlantic City to do some gambling between playoff games. Look, the man knows his body. He knows what he can and can't do. I'm a little bit like Jordan. I like to go out, stay late, and have a good time, but I don't drink, and I don't come home feeling all tired and strung out. It's the same with Michael.

And then the guy came out with the book about how Jordan owed him a million dollars in golfing bets. I don't care how much he owed him, it's nobody's business except Michael's. Jordan makes a lot of money and if a guy wants to play cards and golf for money, so what? Personally, my idea of gambling is to bet a friend ten dollars on a video game, then not even collect if I win. (Or pay if I don't.) But if I felt like gambling, if that's how I had fun, then I would do it, and it should be the same for Michael.

He's also gotten in trouble with some people in the black community because they say he doesn't do enough for them. I know something about that. I already know that some blacks look at me and say, "Hey, he's forgotten where he came from." When I hired Leonard Armato to be my attorney, I heard people say, "Oh, you should've gotten a black lawyer." But I'm going to hire the person who's going to get the job done for me, whether he's black, white, or green. I learned a long time ago that if you can't control something, then you shouldn't worry about it. You can't please everybody, especially when you're out in the public spotlight like Jordan.

When I was at LSU somebody asked me what I felt about David Duke, the ex-Ku Klux Klan guy who was running for governor. They wanted to know if the recruiting of black athletes would be hurt if he won the election. I don't like political questions. I don't consider myself a political expert. But all I said was that a high school kid should be able to make his decision based on what he liked about the college and what he, liked about the coach, not who was governor of the state. So, the Duke people went out and announced that Shaquille O'Neal said a David Duke victory in the governor's race would have no negative effects. Sometimes you have to answer what people say about you and this was one of the times. I went to my coach, Dale Brown, and we worked on a statement that denied what the Duke people were trying to say. The worst thing was some of my friends actually believed I was for David Duke because people tend to believe what they read, not what someone's telling them right to their face. Some people busted the headlights in my car and put Duke stickers all over it.

Jordan must deal with that kind of stuff every day, people trying to get him on their side of one issue or another.

What happened with Jordan's image is that society set him up to be perfect, then tore him down when he wasn't. Maybe some of that was Michael's fault because his commercials built him up too much. I thought about that. I didn't want to turn myself into some kind of superhero who didn't seem real. In my Reebok commercial I rip down a basket, but I also get a dustpan to pick up the pieces. In my Pepsi commercial I bend down a rim, but I also get dissed by a little kid. Maybe Michael should've done more of that in the beginning. But who knew that? Look, Michael Jordan doesn't do drugs, he's a real person, he's accomplished a lot, he's a good man, he treats his mom, his dad, his wife, and his kids real nice. That's what's important.

But people still want a piece of him, and I was getting to know that feeling. One day during the season I suddenly started getting a bunch of phone calls from little kids at my home. It turned out that somebody had gotten my number and put it up on a school bulletin board. I wonder how many times Jordan has had to change his number. Another day I was filling up my car at a gas station in Orlando and I was in a hurry. This woman rushed up to me and told me to sign an autograph. I told her I was off that day and left the station. But she followed me all the way to the Hard Rock Café where I was meeting someone to talk about a business deal. She comes in, interrupts me, and insists that I sign. I said, "I told you once nice, and the answer is still no." So she says to me, "Enjoy your millions, buddy," and walks off.

Now, just because I have a million-dollar salary that means she *owns* me? That's the kind of stuff Jordan's been dealing with for years.

Sometimes people just want to provoke you into doing something, so, if you beat them up or get into some kind of hollering match or something, they can make money off you. As long as someone doesn't try to harm me or my family, they can say what they want. And think about it: you ever read an article about Jordan getting in trouble in public by reacting to something someone said? Never. That's self-control.

A lot of people go after you because of jealousy. And not just fans. One of the things that bothered me about my rookie year was the jealousy about my contract, jealousy about me making the All-Star team ahead of some veterans, jealousy about my endorsements. I know for a fact that's how a lot of players in the league feel about Jordan. But he wasn't one of them. You might think he would've had some bad things to say about me, but he didn't. And then he goes out of his way to visit me, to show me respect, kind of like welcome me into the league. That's class.

We weren't great friends or anything like that. We met for the first time when I was being recruited by Dean Smith at North Carolina. I went down to Chapel Hill for my campus visit on the night the Bulls were playing the Cleveland Cavaliers in a preseason game. I shook his hand in the locker room, and he made a typical Jordan comment. "If you come here," he told me, "I'm gonna dunk on your head in the summer." He was talking about the famous pickup games they played in Chapel Hill, and I wish I would've had the chance to take him up on it. But I didn't want to go to North Carolina and play in the ACC. Don't get me wrong—they play great basketball in that conference. But I liked that roughneck, countryboy image that LSU and the Southeastern Conference had. That was more me.

The connection between Jordan and other young players like me is that we have to pick up where Jordan left off. He used to be the one traveling around the country, answering question after question, night after night, always promoting the NBA, always putting people in the seats. He still does it, but he's gotten a little tired of it. I can see why, because I'm tired of it and I've only done it for a season. But when it's all said and done, I think Michael Jordan has done a great job.

• • •

In the locker room before the Bulls' game that next night, I really didn't think much about Michael on an individual basis. The man I had to check, most of the time anyway, was going to be Bill Cartwright, an old pro who knew a lot of tricks. Cartwright had told a Chicago reporter that from what he had seen of me, I liked to "crash into guys and shoot the ball." Well, what I heard about Cartwright was the same thing. That was okay—bring him on.

But Jordan's the kind of guy who's always on your mind because of the potential for embarrassment. One of the things you think about is that maybe he'll throw down one of those tongue-out, legs-spread, bald-head-glistenin' dunks on you, and next thing you know you're on a Jordan poster or a Jordan calendar or a Jordan video commercial, ducking out of the way and looking stupid. I didn't need that. Not the Shaq Attack.

The other thing about the Bulls is that there's lots of other good players on that team, like Scottie Pippen, Horace Grant, and B. J. Armstrong. And they play well together, too. We don't have that kind of team chemistry out on the court in Orlando, maybe because we're young. It takes time. But once we learn each other's game, and everybody comes to accept their role, the Orlando Magic is going to win it all. It took Michael seven years to get his first ring, and he might be the greatest player ever.

One of the things I wanted for this game was to bring my twelve-year-old brother Jamal to town to be a Magic ballboy. We took a couple photos at center court before the game, just Michael and me, and I made sure that Jamal got into one. I had Alex Martins, the Magic's public relations director, get Michael to sign a couple of basketball cards for me, too. That's not unusual. Lots of players exchange sneakers, cards, whatever. I'm starting a sports room at home and Jordan's card is going to be right up there, under glass, along with my Ken Griffey Jr. baseball, my Muhammad Ali boxing gloves, my Mario Lemieux jersey, my Barry Bonds bat.

The Bulls weren't playing real well at the time, or, at least, that's what everybody was saying about them. They had a record of 23–10. Meanwhile, we were 14–14 and supposedly having a pretty good season. That's the difference between a team that won 67 games and a championship the year before and a team that won only 21 games, like the Magic did before I came.

I'll tell you about the whole game later on, but what sticks out in my mind is the opening tap and the first possession. I walked out there and all of a sudden it hit me—I was on the court with Jordan. I could remember being in high school and watching him and wondering if I'd ever get the chance to stick him. And there it was. On our first possession, the ball came into me and I went up for a shot. Out of the corner of my eye, I saw a flash of red and black come across the lane. As I went up, this flash managed to get my shot, cleanly, from the side. I think I saw the flash smile a little bit, too. I think I saw a 23 on his jersey. And I wondered if that flash hadn't been out there on the golf course the day before, looking at my house, smiling, and just knowing what he was going to do the first time I touched the ball.

I thought to myself, "When you play against Michael, bro, you know you're in the big leagues."

CHAPTER TWO

Gettin'
Whupped into
Line

My birth weight was 7 pounds, 11 ounces, two lucky numbers as my mother used to say. But for the first eleven or twelve years of my life, I don't think my parents thought they were very lucky. Looking back, I don't know why they didn't kill me before I became a teenager. Well, actually my father almost did. And if he had, they would've called it justifiable homicide.

I really don't know why I was such a bad kid. A psychologist would've looked at my boyhood and said, "Well, he didn't react well to all that moving around," but I don't buy that. There was always a lot of love in our house, but it didn't seem to be enough for me. I was always trying to get attention and so I acted like a juvenile delinquent. I never killed anyone or did drugs or anything like that, but I was bad.

I lived the first few years of my life in Newark N.J., where my father, Philip Harrison, and my mother, Lucille O'Neal, both worked for the city. Littleton Avenue, where we lived, wasn't the worst neighborhood around but they wouldn't have filmed any "Cosby" episodes there, either. The race riots of the late-Sixties took place nearby, and the saying was, if you concentrated real hard, you could still smell the smoke from all the fires.

My father joined the army when I was two, so he could make a better living and also so he could get us out of the 'hood. I was born two years before my parents were married. To keep my mother's last name going, they made me an O'Neal. My mother wanted me to have a first name that was unique and, one day, when she looking through a book of Islamic names, she came upon it. Shaquille Rashuan, which means "Little Warrior." I was never very little but I was always a warrior. At first I didn't like my name but then I came to see its unique quality, and what a born basketball name it is, and I'm glad they did it. Michael Jordan. Larry Bird. Shaquille O'Neal—basketball names. And it's the kind of name you tend to remember. Later, when I was in college at LSU, I found out that one couple named their first child Shaquille O'Neal Long because they liked the sound of my name so much.

When I got to school age we moved to Jersey City into a big, old seven-room house at 100 Oak St. that belonged to my mother's mother, Odessa. My earliest memory is thinking that that house was haunted, and I used to get scared lying there in the dark. But I'll tell you what was worse—my school was directly across the street. That was real spooky.

I was a sneaky kid. My mother and grandmother used to hide extra bottles in my room, and I was the kind of kid that used to hunt them down and drink them. One day I spotted one of my teddy bears and a lighter at the same time. Teddy bear. Lighter. Now, I'm thinking that I'm just going to burn him a little bit, then put him out, but as soon as I lit him—poof!—he went up. The room got all smokey and I heard my mom yelling, "What are you doing up there?" So I threw the bear under the bed and she came in.

"Where'd that smoke come from?" she said.

"Oh, that's from outside," I said.

She didn't buy it.

The outcome? I got a whuppin'.

When I was halfway through first grade my father got transferred and we moved to Bayonne, N.J. That was the first time we actually lived on an army base and for the next eleven years, until I went away to college at LSU, that's how I was raised. I really don't know what my life would have been like if I had stayed in big cities. I know my mother and father would've been on me, but there were a lot more temptations—drugs, gangs, weapons. Late in my third grade we moved from Bayonne to Eatontown, N.J., and, halfway through my fifth grade, we moved to Fort Stewart, Georgia.

By that time a pattern had been established. I'd come into a new place, I'd get teased about my name (sometimes they'd call me Sha-Queer) or my size and how I must've flunked a couple grades, and I'd bash somebody in the face. It took a while to gain friends because kids just naturally thought I was mean, which was a logical conclusion because I was big, always fighting, and cursing out teachers. But I wasn't mean. I was a follower, doing things just because they seemed to be cool.

Once, when we were living in Bayonne, I went up to this fire alarm on the base that my father had told me not to mess around with. So, naturally, I pulled it, the MPs caught me, and hauled me into their station. Then they called my dad. "I'll be right there," he said.

So my dad came walking into the station holding one of those racquetball paddles, the ones with the big holes, and the bad news was there were no courts nearby.

"Phil," one of the MPs said, "if you hit your boy with

that racquet, we're gonna arrest you right on the spot.''

"Then start filling out the papers," my dad said, "because I'm gonna tear his butt up.'' He did, too. And I never pulled another fire alarm.

One of the things my father used to do was walk up to school unannounced to see what I was up to. You could call this "sneaking around," but my father, being an army dude, would call it "a reconnaissance mission." Anyway, on one of those missions he peered in a window and happened to see me strutting around, my shirt all unbuttoned, showing off this big necklace I was wearing, acting just like a big goof. And he wailed me right there.

My father's weapon of choice was his hand because I was too big for the strap. One time I managed to get my forearm up to protect myself and—whap!—he practically broke his hand. I can still see him grimacing, pretending that it didn't hurt, while my mother tried to keep from laughing.

In general, my mother, being the soft one, didn't hit me. We had a very orderly system, and my mom's duties were to keep the house and cook, and my dad's duties were to win the bread and beat his son into line. But even my mother had her limits. One day when I was pretty young she dressed me all in white for a school program and sat me down beside her. Sure enough, pretty soon I jumped off my seat and started crawling around on the floor, between the seats, just bothering everybody and making a nuisance out of myself. She scooped me up, ran out the door, took me home, and, unfortunately, handed me over to my father.

But my mother didn't like weakness either. Early on in Jersey City, back when I was the beaten instead of the beater, I would run in the house crying after a kid picked on me, and my mother would say, "You truck right on back there and take care of business." There was a kid named Pee Wee who used to mess with me all the time. I didn't like to fight him because he had a big, nasty German shepherd named Sam as his backup. One day I just got tired of Pee Wee's stuff and I

punched him in the nose hard, blood spilling all over the place.
Later on, a bunch of us were playing basketball in the park—I
remember I had on these old Chuck Taylor sneakers—and all
of a sudden we heard Sam coming from off in the distance,
barking that mean bark, and we all said, "Whoa, man, here
comes Sam!" And we beat it out of there.

Once I got older, though, I was usually instigating the fights.
One thing I used to hate was tattle-tales, and I used to sit in
class and throw spitballs at them. The teacher used to say,
"Who did that?" and the tattle-tales would tell on me again. It
was an endless cycle. But something happened when I was in
sixth grade in Georgia that changed my fighting career. I told
one of the tattle-tales I was going to beat him up after school
and I had my boys waiting for him in case he tried to sneak out.
We waited for two hours until he finally came out the door of
the school and tried to make a run for it. We all had jackets
printed with WARRIORS. It wasn't like a real gang, but we
thought we were pretty cool. Anyway, I caught this kid and
started punching him again and again, in his stomach and
face, and all of a sudden he went into sort of a seizure. A guy
passing by knew enough to slip something under his tongue. I
wouldn't say I never got into a street fight after that, but I
thought twice about it.

One of the hardest things that my parents had to deal with
was my dancing ability. I was really good at it, never clumsy,
never handicapped by my size, and I think they were secretly
proud of me. I probably inherited the ability from my mother,
who's a very graceful woman. Anyway, break-dancing was big
when I was in school and I used to get right down to it whenever the spirit moved me. The shiny hallways in the school
were good places and so were the floors in wood shop that
were covered with sawdust. Some teachers appreciated my
ability, others didn't think school was the place for dancing,
and others didn't know what the heck I was trying to do. One
time my parents came in for a conference and this teacher
called them over and whispered, "Listen, does Shaquille have

any trouble with seizures? The other day I walked out in the hall and he was down on the floor squirming around with a big crowd of students watching him." I guess the guy wasn't a fan of *Soul Train*. I used to tell everyone that I wanted to be a professional dancer like the kids on *Fame,* which was one of my favorite TV shows. But I really never thought it would happen after I started growing. There just aren't many dancers my size.

The fact that I was good at it, though, demonstrates that I have rhythm, which is something a lot of 'footers—that's my word for seven-footers—don't have. I don't think Bill Laimbeer, for example, did much dancing when he was young. Patrick Ewing looks graceful, though, and so does Hakeem Olajuwon.

When I was in sixth grade our family made the big move—to Germany. It was hard for me; I didn't want to go. We were always packing up just as I was beginning to make friends and each year it got harder. Some kids I didn't miss, like Pee Wee and his damn dog, but I had real good friends in Georgia, two guys named Eric McNeal and Rodney Philpot. Since then, I've totally lost track of them. Eric and Rodney, if you're reading this, give me a holler.

Germany was hard to get used to, particularly since a lot of time we lived up in the mountains where it was cold. It was strange there sometimes. There were a lot of threats from terrorists, and a lot of security measures because some American personnel in Berlin had been killed when a bunch of Libyans blew up a disco. Every once in a while some German radicals would get on the base and paint American tanks blue as some kind of protest that at the time I really didn't understand. The army kids tended to hang together. I went to school with a lot of officers' children. My dad did pretty well as a supply sergeant, but I never had the new bike to ride to school or the real nice house to live in. I used to be jealous. I'll admit it. I told myself, "I'm going to be rich someday, richer than these kids." Sometimes wishes come true.

The rumor among the army kids in Germany was that if your parents couldn't handle you, they'd send you back to the States. I hated Germany at first, so I did everything in my power to make my father send me back. I will say with some pride that I never got into drugs and alcohol. There were kids doing drugs, even on the army base, but it just wasn't for me. I was always scared of dying from some kind of overdose. Or, worse yet, having my father find out I was doing drugs and dying an even more painful slow death. Same thing with booze. I took a sip of beer once and the only word I can find for it is "nasty." I don't like the taste of it, and I don't like what it does to you. I can act stupid on my own if I care to—I don't need help.

But I did everything else wrong to try to get back to the U.S. I'd beat people up, hit teachers, spit on people, break into cars and take tapes. I was a real jerk but I thought I was cool. In fact, my nickname among the other kids was J.C.—Just Cool.

But nothing swayed my father. And one day he sat me down and said: "Look, son, no matter what you do, I'm not letting them send you back. And if you don't listen to me I'm going to beat your butt. Every . . . single . . . day."

I can't say if it was that speech that got me turned around. It was probably a combination of things. I got tired of the beatings for one thing. And I came to realize that it was better to get rewarded than punished. See, my parents weren't the kind of people to just discipline me for no reason. They went after me when I was bad, but they praised me when I did good. My father beat me for the last time when I was in eighth grade, thirteen years old. I'm not saying I never screwed up after that, but I pretty much toed the line.

What turned me around the most, I guess, was sports, and once again I have my father to thank. In between fooling around, getting suspended, and getting whupped by the sergeant, athletics took up most of my time.

My father had been a pretty good athlete himself, mostly basketball and football, where he grew up around Newark.

One of his claims to fame was getting his teeth knocked out by Dave Cowens, the former Celtic center, in a pickup game in East Orange. My dad always liked Cowens after that. He likes guys who knock people's teeth out, as long as it wasn't done dirty.

I was about seven or eight when I first started playing basketball, and my father was my first coach. He can still get out that photo of our base team and name every kid on it. He was a fundamentals-oriented coach. We ran the old Boston Celtic offense, although the only reason I knew that was because he used to tell me. All those old plays. He'd have me pop out at the top of the key and look inside to make the pass. He didn't want me standing under the basket and taking easy shots just because I was taller than everyone else.

I played football on the base teams, too, and even for a little while in Germany. I was a tailback, and if you don't think the defense got a little worried when this monster of a kid came bearing down on them, think again. I finally gave it up one cold day in Germany when I got chopped at the knees about a dozen times in a row. I stood up, dusted myself off, left the field, took off my pads, and said: "That's it." It was a good move. There's not much of a market for seven-foot-tall tailbacks.

The more I practiced basketball, the better I got, and the further it kept me away from trouble. My father's lessons were simple: work hard, concentrate, be mentally tough, be persistent. His work ethic, the kind of person he was, came through in the way he coached me in sports. I didn't begin to appreciate it until later. He was always looking for a way to make things better for us. Before we went to Germany, where he was pretty busy around the base being a supply sergeant, I remember him sometimes working three jobs—the army job, driving trucks back and forth from New York to Jersey, and shining shoes or selling hats. Whatever he had to do to make life comfortable for us, he did it. I can remember him going from bank to bank asking, "Look, loan me money. I'm a good risk. I'll pay you back.'' Sometimes they did, sometimes they turned him down, but he kept at it. He's a strong man, and he always tried to transfer that strength to me on the basketball court. *Your ball, your court, your game.* That's what he used to tell me. That was his credo. Nothing else mattered if you were a player. I remember one time in Germany I had jheri-curls and an earring. I don't think my father liked it too much, and even I got tired of it and gave it up because I had to put this activator juice in my hair every night. But because I was getting down to business, listening to his lessons, and working hard, he didn't say anything about it.

You're probably thinking that it's easy to dominate when you're the tallest kid around, but that wasn't always the way it was. For one thing, I was embarrassed about my height for quite a while and I'd slouch around trying to make myself look shorter. That begins to act on you mentally, too, and you begin, in a way, to *play* shorter. My parents told me to be proud of my size but I wasn't. I wanted to be normal. For another thing, I was really bothered by Osgood-Schlatter's disease, which really caused me a lot of pain in my knees, particularly since I was growing so fast. I had to take calcium pills, drink a lot of milk, and eat bananas to try to counteract it, but it really didn't go away until I got to high school. That definitely slowed my basketball progress. I remember that even though I was 6'7" or 6'8" by the time I was fourteen, I couldn't dunk. No matter how hard I tried, I couldn't do it. Then one day it just happened. It was a real weak dunk but it was a dunk, and I ran off the court yelling to all my friends to come watch me dunk. I rounded up a few of them, brought them back to the court, and then got humiliated when I couldn't do it again.

It was about this time, when I was just starting to develop in basketball and really take an interest in it, that I met Dale Brown who later became my coach at LSU. There's been so many stories about how me met in Germany that I'm going to give you the whole thing just as it happened.

I was thirteen years old and I guess my father was already thinking about getting me into college. He came into my room one day and said, "Hey, there's this American college coach giving a clinic down at the gym. Maybe you should go check him out." My father himself was on his way to relax at the sauna, which I thought was a much better idea than going to see some college coach I never heard of. But he kept at it, and when my father kept at something, I pretty much got the message that I should go.

Anyway, I got a seat in the front row and I remember Coach Brown was talking about shooting. He said, "When you shoot, your arm has to be straight." He told us he could come close to making a three-quarters-of-the-court-length shot almost every time just because of proper arm position. "Who wants to try it?" he asked, and then our eyes met. "Here, you, young fella, get the ball and try." I threw it, hit the rim, and he said, "Good shot."

That might've been the end of it except that he got me thinking, and so I pulled him aside after he finished signing autographs and said, "Look, I'm 6'8". I've got bad knees and I can't dunk. Could you give me a weight program so I can develop my legs? I just want to become a good player."

So he showed me a basic Nautilus program, gave me a brochure or something, and asked me: "How long you been in the army, soldier?"

"I'm not in the army," he said. "I'm only thirteen."

He couldn't believe it. "You on the high school basketball team?" he asked me.

"No," I told him. "I'm not good enough."

That was too much for Coach Brown. "Where's your father?" he said. "You're gonna be a seven-footer easily." And off we went to the sauna.

My father didn't waste much time making a lasting impression. Coach Brown got about two seconds into his recruiting speech when my father raised his hand and said, "Coach, I'm not trying to be rude. But I'm not all that interested in hearing about basketball. Tell me about how you want to help my son make something of himself beyond basketball. It's about time black kids started thinking about becoming presidents of corporations instead of blue-collar workers, head coaches instead of assistants, generals instead of sergeants." That line of thinking appealed to Coach Brown and they exchanged cards and addresses. I really never thought anything would come of it, though. And it may not have if I had stayed in Germany for all four years of high school. I wouldn't have developed as a player and even a persistent guy like Coach Brown might've forgotten about me.

But in the spring of my sophomore year my father once again got transferred, this time back to the States, to San Antonio, Texas. I was an American again, and it felt great, not to mention what it did for my basketball career.

When I think back to those early years of moving around and the times I was unhappy in various places, I can also see the other side of the coin. You learn things as an army brat that you don't even know you're learning. The discipline, for one thing. If you screw up—and, man, did I screw up—you face the consequences. With my dad, there was no, "Well, we'll let it go this time." He didn't let *anything* go. And, gradually, you learn how to behave, how to respect authority. Also, I think service kids are a little more socially aware than other kids. We made friends easier and quicker and adapted to new situations, simply because we had to. It was a survival tool. Even today, if you ask my mother where home is, she'll say, "Home is wherever we're living." And if you ask me, I'll say, "Home is where my mother is."

A little later, when I was in high school, I remember I was on a search for role models—Michael Jordan, Magic Johnson, people like that. Then I hit upon it one day that I really didn't have to look that far. My parents were my role models. All I had to do was pattern myself after them. You know what I'm thankful they taught me? The little things. The little things that make people happy and show that you're a considerate person. I remember later on when I got to San Antonio I climbed into my coach's car after a game, and, before I sat down, I put a towel on the seat so I wouldn't stain anything. That coach thought that was so nice that he told my father about it. "Well," my dad said, "I would hope he did that. That's how we brought him up."

Later on in the year my father got in a couple scrapes with people, one of them with a writer who was doing an unauthorized book on me. Some people don't understand my father, understand his approach. He's an army guy who's used to giving and taking orders, and he hollers a lot. He approaches situations aggressively. He's blunt. But he's got a side of him that no one knows about. There was a letter in an Orlando newspaper late in the season about a mother and son who ran into a big black man at the Magic team store. The little boy was looking at a poster of me, and the next thing he knew the man was arranging to have it sent overnight to the boy's house. Only as they were leaving the store did the attendant tell them that the man was my father. He does stuff like that all the time. But you don't always read about it in the newspaper.

I'm glad my dad whupped me into line. When he has a problem at home now, with either of my younger sisters, LaTeefah or Ayesha, or my brother Jamal, he gets me on the phone and I have to talk to them. I always say to my dad: "Bro, you're getting soft." Thank God he wasn't soft when I was growing up.

CHAPTER THREE

Summer in the City

Did I want to play for the Los Angeles Lakers?

Man, what do you think? Of course I did. The Lakers were the Lakers. They had tradition, but they weren't old and musty like the Boston Celtics. They had Magic Johnson, the Laker Girls, the Forum, Jack Nicholson hangin' at the sideline, Hollywood, Beverly Hills, the beach. When I was in college at LSU, we wore purple and gold uniforms, same as the Lakers, so that would've been a natural. And I wanted to play there even more after spending a lot of the summer of 1992 in Los Angeles, chillin' at the clubs, talking about deals with my agent, Leonard Armato, playing ball with Magic at UCLA, working one-on-one with Hakeem Olajuwon at some dumpy high school gym with no cameras, no spectators, no hype, only sweat and hard work.

But, and this is a big but, did I ever say the Lakers were the *only* team I'd play for? Never. After I declared for the draft in April 1992, right after I finished my junior season at LSU, somebody asked me where I'd like to play in the NBA. Right away I said L.A., and I was talking more about the Lakers than the Clippers. Next thing I knew, it was getting around that "Shaquille's only gonna play for the Lakers." Not the case. I'm a realist, bro. Since they had made the playoffs the year before and wouldn't be in the lottery, the Lakers were not going to get me. Simple as that.

I'll be honest with you, though, Leonard's first thought was that I should play in L.A. Right after I hired him as my representative, my dad and I asked him to prepare kind of a prospectus of my future. We wanted to see things like a marketing plan, his ideas about public relations, and what he projected as my image as an NBA player. And one of the pages in Leonard's outline was called "How to Orchestrate a Trade to Los Angeles." (The Magic people might've had a heart attack if they had seen that after they won the lottery.)

He had the plan worked out so it made a lot of sense. First, I would sign major deals like shoes and trading cards to provide financial security in the event that I had to sit out one or two years. I would also look into getting a record company or a trading card company going, another security measure, but also to keep my mind occupied if I wasn't playing in the NBA. Tell you the truth, the idea of running a business appealed to me, and I know I'm going to be doing it real soon in any case. Also, I could've signed to play with one of those charitable teams, like Athletes in Action or High Five America, to stay in shape. Or maybe I would've formed my own team. Shaq's Pack. Shaq's Hacks. The Shaq-a-Lacks.

But I was never completely comfortable with the idea of sitting out or demanding a trade. Danny Ferry of the Cavaliers did it a couple years ago because he didn't want to play for the

Clippers, and he landed up basically wasting a year in Italy, eating spaghetti and forgetting how to rebound. Something about it bothered me. I figured I was a player and players played. And I didn't want to start out my NBA career on a negative publicity note as being a selfish guy. But Leonard was right to talk about it. One of the jobs of a representative is to bring all the options to the table. I think the real reason Leonard thought about getting me to the Lakers, though, was because he could just drive the ten miles from Century City, where his office is, to the Forum to watch me play. Now he's got to get on a plane, fly across the country to Orlando, and there's only so many times a guy can visit EPCOT Center and Sea World. Sorry, Leonard.

Hiring Leonard was one of the best moves I made in my rookie year, maybe *the* best. Leonard had played point guard at USC and the University of Pacific for a guy named Stan Morrison—I think that was after the center jump was invented but I'm not sure—who was a good friend of Coach Brown's. Coach Brown was the kind of guy who really didn't like agents much, but Leonard made an impression on him. I first met Leonard when he was down visiting Coach Brown one day during my sophomore year. Coach introduced us and said, "Here's a guy you should consider when you get ready." Tell you the truth, it passed in and out of my mind. I met Leonard again a little while later when I went to the John Wooden Awards in Los Angeles and then I was impressed because he was the only one who didn't come at me with a bunch of promises. You know, "I can get you this, I can get you that." Leonard didn't offer me anything. I knew football players at LSU who would meet up with these agents and they'd come back with brand new cars and a whole bunch of money. I never envied them. I didn't want somebody I didn't know buying me things in exchange for my future. It was like selling your soul to the devil.

When it came time for me to pick an agent, it really wasn't a hard decision for me. Two of the big guys, David Falk of

ProServ, Jordan's agent, and Bob Woolf, Larry Bird's agent, didn't even contact me. I don't know why. Maybe they were scared of negotiating with my father. Anyway, by then Leonard had developed a relationship with my parents, passed the test of fire so to speak, and that counted for a lot. The one guy who really came after me hard was Lance Luchnick, a guy from Chicago whom I didn't want to go with. Lance was like "I can get you this and that." Leonard was like "How are you doing, nice to meet you. I'm sure you're going to be a great athlete." The mistake people made was to think that I was a materialistic person, and that I could be tempted with cars and all that. Didn't work, bro. I looked at Leonard's client list and what impressed me was that it was built on quality, not quantity. He had Ronnie Lott, Ahmad Rashad, Hakeem Olajuwon, and Sinjin Smith, a pro beach volleyball player I used to watch on ESPN. I figured Shaquille Rashuan O'Neal fit in there real nice.

Anyway, by the time of the lottery drawing, in May 1992, I had pretty much ruled out the idea of trying to orchestrate a trade. Myself, Leonard, and Dennis Tracey, my roommate at LSU whom I had hired as my personal assistant, watched the lottery at Leonard's house in L.A. I tried to keep my mind blank, but, okay, I'll let you in on a secret, bro—I felt some serious relief when Minnesota didn't get the top pick. They finished third and later took Christian Laettner. I've got nothing against Minnesota, nothing against a Timberwolf, nothing against anyone in their organization. But I do have something against wearing a snowsuit for eight months of the year. I'm not totally sure what Leonard and I would've done if Minnesota would've gotten the first pick. But I probably would've picked up that prospectus and read the section called "Orchestrating a Trade . . ." a little more closely. Or I might be a Timberwolf and be totally happy in Minnesota, maybe learning how to ice fish or something. I'm not sure.

I wasn't being cocky when I assumed I'd be the first pick. Ever since my sophomore year people like Marty Blake, the

NBA's chief scout, and commentators like Dick Vitale and Mike Fratello were saying that I would be No. 1 whenever I came out. Anyway, Pat Williams, the general manager of the Magic, had a Shaq jersey right there at the lottery, and he later told me that there were ten other teams with Shaq jerseys all ready, too. I didn't know that. I wondered whether a team that already had a good center would go for a point guard or something if they got the first pick. In the draft, I don't think the best player gets picked number one all the time.

Eventually, it came down to Charlotte and Orlando, and it didn't make much difference to me. I was pretty good friends with Larry Johnson, the top pick in the 1991 draft, and I knew we'd be able to tear it up if I got picked by the Hornets. But Orlando seemed like a nice place, too—warm weather, friendly people from what I'd heard, and a couple of good, young players like Nick Anderson and Dennis Scott. And then they turned over Charlotte's card for the No. 2 spot and that meant I was going to Orlando. I remember Pat Williams looked like a cat who swallowed a canary. Just a few days later, the Magic offices were already playing a song called "Love Shack" by the B-52s over their telephone system. The B-52s aren't really my style—if I would've had time, maybe I would've written a rap song for them. *Shaq is comin/Y'all take heart/Shaq is comin/Get a brand new start.*

I felt good about the choice. The only minor worry I had about the Magic was that, at the time, they had Stanley Roberts, my old teammate from LSU. It wasn't anything personal about Stan, who was a pretty good friend. But we're both centers, and I couldn't see a Twin Tower thing working. Stan, I would've hated to come down there and taken your job, but some things can't be helped.

The draft wasn't until June 24, a month later in Portland, Oregon, and Leonard and I decided just to chill until then. We didn't have anything to gain by talking one way or the other about Orlando. I left that strategy, all the no-comments and the like, up to Leonard and went on with my business. I saw what a media circus my rookie year was going to be, though, when I went to the NBA's rookie camp in Chicago a few weeks before the draft. When I walked into the lobby of the hotel, there were four camera crews ready to pounce on me. Before I knew it, the lights were on and they were asking me if it was true that I wasn't going to play for Orlando. I basically told them that in a perfect world I'd play for the Lakers, but the world wasn't perfect.

That was also the first time I met Alex Martins, the public relations director for the Magic. Alex came up to me, introduced himself, and talked about how we'd have to work closely together to handle all the interview requests. That turned out to be the understatement of the year.

All along, the Magic were hoping they could get me down to Orlando before the draft to put on a big show and convince me that I should sign with them. I'm not much for big shows, but Leonard and I felt it would be a good idea just to see how serious they were about signing me. And, man, they were serious. We arranged the trip on June 18, six days before the draft. My father and Jamal came along and they took real good care of us. They sent a private plane to pick us up in San Antonio. There were about one hundred people waiting for us at the airport. The team owner, Richard DeVos was there, along with Pat Williams and all the Magic executives. We drove right to the team store and my dad all but cleaned them out of hats and T-shirts. He kept calling back to San Antonio from the limo reporting what was going on to my mom. We drove to Pat Williams's house and left Jamal there to play with Pat's sixteen kids. We toured the Arena, had dinner, met the press. The people were nice, the city was nice, the weather was nice. Right away, I saw that I could be happy there.

But the best thing was, right away, you could see they weren't—excuse my language—bullshitting around. They said, "Shaq, we want you, we don't want you sitting out half the year and all that junk. Whatever you want, whatever we want, we're going to come to terms and we're going to come to terms fast. We're business people and I know you, your family, and Leonard are business people, and we don't want you sitting out, because we have the opportunity to do something big here.''

I had a lot of people out in Los Angeles telling me that the Magic wouldn't be able to sign because of the NBA's salary cap, and I wasn't sure myself. The cap is so complicated that somebody could study it for five years and still not understand it. Pat Williams, in fact, talks about having a "capologist" on call to deal with contracts. But I told Leonard right at the beginning: "Don't be foolin' around. Let's get it done so I can play ball.''

Anyway, six days later I was in Portland with my family, and David Stern, the NBA commissioner, was saying, "Good evening, and welcome to the NBA draft. The Orlando Magic have the first pick." I wasn't real nervous because, unless they flew me down to Orlando just because they think I'm good-looking, I knew what was going to happen. A team gets five minutes to announce its pick and at least two went by before Commissioner Stern came back to the microphone. Nobody could figure out what the delay was for and there was kind of a buzz in the room. *Hey, maybe they're trying to trade Shaq.* No, it turned out that, back in Orlando, the Magic were having their own draft show for about ten thousand people at the Arena, and Pat Williams was trying to arrange a real dramatic announcement. He wanted his voice to come through both in Portland and Orlando saying, "The Orlando Magic are pleased to select with the first pick of the 1992 draft Shaquille O'Neal," but he couldn't get the phone line to work. I found out later that he was back there frantically pushing all these buttons and breaking into a cold sweat when Alex Martins simply picks up a remote phone, calls Portland, and says, "Tell the commissioner we're taking Shaq, guys."

Then David Stern announced it, and, well, there I was. Number One. I hadn't been the college player of the year and my team hadn't won an NCAA championship. But nobody could ever take this away from me. When I have children one day, I can put them on my knee, and say, "Son, or daughter, I was The Man in college basketball. They picked me first."

We flew back to Orlando the following night and the next day the Magic really put on a show. A big airport welcome with fans, balloons, the Magic dancers, flags. I felt like Mickey Mouse coming to Fantasy Land, so I put on a pair of mouse ears, and that drove everybody crazy. All those tourists with argyle socks must've wondered what was going on. We went to a press briefing, met the mayor, went to some big community luncheon with hundreds of people there. All the way through this whole thing, remember, I had really not said I was coming to Orlando. I wanted to be cool about it, make sure no big trade was going to happen at the last minute, see where they were coming from. My line had always been, "I just wanna play ball." Finally, at the luncheon, I said: "I just wanna play ball . . . in Orlando." The place went crazy. That was the first time they really knew for sure I was coming.

When it was all said and done, we were comfortable about it, even Leonard. One thing about the NBA that we realized very quickly—it's become so big that it doesn't matter as much as it used to where you play. You could be playing in Sheboygan, and, if you're good enough, they'll find you, write about you, talk about you. It was similar to the situation when my family moved from Germany to San Antonio before my junior year in high school. Everybody was telling me that I had to go to a big high school instead of to Robert G. Cole High, the one that was right on the army base.

"Don't listen to that garbage," my father told me. "If you're good enough, they'll find you." He was right.

Leonard and the Magic people started negotiating right away and my father and I sat in on the first couple sessions. But by this time I was getting tired of all the hype, all the talk, all the applause, all the pats on the back. I wanted to get back to San Antonio and Los Angeles and spend the rest of the summer working out and finding some time to relax before my professional career started. I patted Leonard on the back and said, "Get it done, bro. And hurry up please."

● ● ●

I hung around San Antonio for a while but it was hard getting in good runs on the army base. There just aren't a lot of 'footers in the army, and I'd play with guys 6'2" or 6'3", and it wasn't doing me a lot of good because no one could bang with me. It would've been nice if the Spurs' David Robinson had been around—then we could've gone a little Army versus Navy—but he was off doing commercials. So I decided to spend most of my time in L.A.

I liked the city right away, and, had it worked out for me to play for the Lakers, I would've felt right at home. I could've bought a big, showoff-type house for the summer but instead I rented a little two-room place at Oakwood Apartments, right off Sepulveda Boulevard. I knew I wasn't going to be doing much in it besides sleeping.

I had been out there for the Wooden Awards in March and met Magic Johnson for the first time at a Laker game through our agents. We just shook hands and talked a couple minutes because, like I said, I don't like to bother people in public. A couple days later, Magic called Leonard with this message. "Hey, me and some of my boys are runnin' tomorrow morning at UCLA. Can Shaq come over at nine?"

Yeah, Shaq could come over. Matter of fact, Shaq could be there by eight.

I was, too. I got over to Pauley Pavilion at UCLA before the janitor, and I was shooting around when Magic showed up at nine. Nobody could believe I was there because Magic prided himself on showing up first. Magic had retired by then—this was about six months after he first announced he was HIV-positive—but he was trying to stay in shape for the Olympics and he looked great. He said to me, "Good luck, you made a good decision coming out this year, and good luck in the league." Then we got down to playing.

I'm not gonna make too much of summer pickup games, I don't care whether Magic Johnson, Michael Jordan, and Larry Bird are playing. But I'm not gonna make too little of them, either. I was playing against guys who had been in the league for a long time, guys like Hakeem, James Edwards, A.C. Green and the Magic Man himself. They banged a lot, and, when they saw I could take their banging, they knew I was going to come in and do pretty well. And I knew it, too. There was a couple minutes before that first game when I was a little nervous. But I quickly saw I could hold my own. In a way, in fact, the summer games are more of a pure basketball test because there's no refs and there's a kind of code of honor that you play hard and physical but not dirty. That's my kind of game, and, in the NBA, the refs don't always let you play it. Right, Darell Garretson?

Eventually, later in the summer, Magic invited me to play in his charity game. By that time, I had gotten a lot of press and I had the feeling that some guys were trying to outdo me. Fine. But my shots were falling, I was having a good game, and I finished with thirty-six points. Like most exhibitions, there wasn't much defense being played, and Arsenio Hall was my coach, so it wasn't like I was getting it confused with a real game. Still, I played well, and, by that time, I knew I would do okay in the NBA. That didn't mean I wasn't nervous before my first official test, as you'll see, but I knew I belonged.

Magic is a really special person. He talked to me, gave me some advice about fame, especially about not becoming a hermit and turning myself into Elvis. I don't really have an opinion about whether or not he should've kept playing. He made the choice he felt he had to make and that's that. I never talked about AIDS with him because I think he had enough people talking about it for him. But I do know that I never worried about playing with him or against him, about knock-

ing him down when he came through the lane. I did my research and came to the conclusion that it's a million to one
shot that you can catch the virus through contact on a basketball court. Some people would say that even those odds aren't
large enough. Fine. You better stay in your house then because
you could get hit by a meteor.

Would I have liked to play against him in the NBA? My
answer is that I played against him, in a pure basketball setting, just ten guys banging and playing, and he still dominated.
Someday I can tell my kids I played against Magic Johnson.
And it doesn't matter that nobody was in the stands.

Another thing that really helped me basketball-wise over the
summer was working out with Hakeem. I naturally developed
a closer relationship with him than anybody else because he's
a client of Leonard's, too, and we'd work out a lot of after-
noons together at Inglewood High School. Hakeem showed
me some moves. He told me what he does in certain situations
and we just talked. If you want to compare me to any athlete,
compare me to Hakeem. He's a great player and a hard
worker, but off the court he's a class act. I think he's the best
center in the league. Jordan's the best player, but he's the best
center. Robinson is pretty quick for his size but Hakeem is
stronger, quicker, and has more moves. Off the court he smiles
all the time, dresses up, takes care of himself, treats people
nice, says hi. A class act. We talked about religion a little bit but
not much. Hakeem's a Muslim and my father is Muslim so I
know something about it. But I didn't get into it that much
because I don't like to talk about things just to talk about them.

A lot of other interesting stuff happened in the summer. Jeff
Hamilton, the designer who makes all those leather coats that
athletes wear, told Magic he wanted to meet me. Normally,
you have to be careful about that kind of request. When I first
went to L.A. there were a lot of people saying, "I wanna do this
for you, I wanna do that for you," and all they really wanted
was something for themselves. But Jeff told Magic, "Tell Shaq
I don't want anything from him. I just want to make him a

coat." So we got together and Jeff showed me a coat that he made for Muhammad Ali.

"Whoa!" I asked him. "You know Ali?"

"Let's go meet him," said Jeff. So we drove down to Ali's house, which is way down by the Mexican border.

Man, I wish my father could've been along for this one. Ali has always been his hero. That may sound funny since my dad's a career army guy and Ali once got in trouble for avoiding the draft. But what he saw in Ali was a black man who stood up for his principles and fought the system when it wasn't a popular thing to do. Also, a guy who worked with Ali went to high school in north Jersey with my father. Ali has his problems, I won't deny that. But he knew who I was, he talked pretty clearly about a lot of things, and he has a sense of humor. He gave me a book and wished me well. Same to you, Muhammad, same to you.

Getting back to the coats—I first had Jeff make one for my parents. And then he made a beautiful leather coat decorated with green Indian beads for one of my sisters. Then I decided I wanted a coat with a Superman emblem on the back. Why not, right? So he made me a short one, and then I told him I wanted the same thing in a trench. Man, that was the coat. Everywhere I went for the first couple months of the season, that's what people talked about. Shaq's Superman coat. It wouldn't have been a good idea to wear it if I had played like Lois Lane, but, by and large, bro, my play matched my coat. Ha, ha, ha.

I did something else important over the summer, too—I kept my commitment to play in Pete Newell's Big Man's Camp when a lot of people thought I'd blow it off. Commitments are to keep—that's why they're called commitments. Pete is kind of like Obi-Wan Kenobi, you know, the old guy in *Star Wars*, who knows everything about everything. That's what Pete is. He's schooled all the great centers at one time or another, and he's a tough guy to please. But I went out there and did a job on most of the other big men, 'footers and all. He liked my shot-blocking timing, my ability to spin right or left, my hands, and especially my attitude. He told me that I've got to acquire technique on offense, some finesse to go with my strength and explosiveness. He's right, too. And I will.

The other thing that happened over the summer was that I helped out my bank account. It seemed that one NBA team, and one shoe company, were pretty happy to get my services.

CHAPTER FOUR

Don't Fake
the Funk

Look, I'm not going to give you every detail about my personal finances. You already know that I get paid $40–$41 million over seven years from the Orlando Magic, and I'm going to tell you about how much I get from Reebok. But if all this book is about is a bunch of figures, and lists of how much money I'm getting from this company and that company, then you're going to get the wrong idea about me. I'm not about money. I'm not about seeing how many cars I can buy, or how many closets I can fill up with clothes. I make more money in one year than my father made in his entire life, but that doesn't make me a better person than him.

In February, ESPN did a show about me called "Shaq's Sudden Impact." It was okay, and I enjoyed talking to all their reporters, but when it came out it was mostly about money, how much I get from this deal, how much I get from that deal, how much money I'll make for this company. It seemed like they were talking about somebody else half the time, some guy who maybe runs an investment company or something.

Anyway, in the world today it's not about making the money, it's about keeping it. I read that the way most million-aires go broke is when they try to make $40 million into $400 million, or take their $400 million and try to turn it into $4 billion. I have a plan. I'm already a millionaire, and I'm just going to invest in low-risk things like C.D.s and government bonds. I arranged with the Magic to get paid every ten days for the whole year. I thought that was a good compromise be-tween once a week and once every two weeks. I don't even see the check, which goes right to my financial adviser. I couldn't blow all my money if I wanted to . . . and I don't want to.

Don't get me wrong—I'm not planning on giving any of the companies any money back. They made an investment in me because they thought it would pay off for them, not because they thought I was such a good-looking guy and they wanted to help me out. It's business. But I don't believe that I person-ally have been changed by the money. I don't think money can change a person. Money can give a person more material items, but people change people. I can turn into a jive-ass nobody just as easily if I'm making ten grand a year as five million.

The bad thing, though, is people *assume* you've changed because now you have money. It's already happened to me. I'll be eating in a restaurant and somebody will ask me for an autograph and I'll turn them down or tell them to wait until I'm finished. But they'll get all upset and say "See, now that he has all this money he's too big to sign autographs." Well, I'm here to tell you that just because I'm a millionaire, I can't enjoy a cheeseburger if I'm being interrupted all the time any more than I could if I was making the minimum wage. The digestive juices don't know the difference.

A lot of people thought that a center, a big guy like myself, wouldn't be able to make much of a living from endorsements. Somebody showed me a clipping of what one guy from Nike said: "There has never in the history of basketball been a center that's been an effective marketing tool. They don't dribble the ball, they don't pass, they don't run. They're primarily in there grabbing the ball and putting it up within five feet of the basket."

That's funny—I seem to remember a few times this season when I dribbled the ball all the way up the court and either passed off or dunked. I seem to remember Hakeem Olajuwon running and Brad Daugherty passing, and I seem to remember Patrick Ewing and David Robinson making a few jumpers from twenty feet. I must've been hallucinating.

But it is true that companies aren't usually willing to give big bucks to the big men. And I think it has more to do with personality than anything else. One of Leonard's clients used to be Kareem Abdul-Jabbar, and he's a kind of an inward guy. I'm an outward guy. Leonard's theory is that most big men keep a distance between themselves and people who are smaller, whether they do it unconsciously or not. But for some reason, despite my size, I'm able to draw people in. I never really thought about it because I'm just who I am, but I guess he's right. Early on, right after I got drafted, Leonard came up with a phrase "Shaquille's a cross between The Terminator and Bambi." Later on, after I tore down a couple baskets, Leonard came up with another one: "Shaq's a superhero who doesn't need special effects." See, that's why I pay Leonard the big bucks.

With all that's happened to me, I really think everybody kind of underestimated me coming out of college. And maybe I underestimated myself, too. I've always been a dreamer, and, from the time I started having real success in basketball, probably about my junior year in high school in San Antonio, I always saw myself being on the front of a cereal box, maybe having a Frosted Flakes commercial. But I don't think anyone really expects companies to be interested in you, not in the beginning.

Right away we could see there was a lot of interest from marketing people, though. There was talk about there being a need for another NBA superstar because Bird was gone and Magic was gone, and Michael was kind of cutting back. But not everybody thought that Shaquille O'Neal, a big center, would be the one to step in.

One of the smartest things we did was create a Shaq Attaq logo for me that could go on all my products. Everybody knows the Air Jordan logo, for example, but that's owned by Nike and can only go on shoes and apparel. My logo can go on all my products, so people can walk into a store and say, "Oh, that's a Shaq shirt" or "That's a Shaq video."

Our first indication that things would be big was trading cards. Once an NBA player has signed his contract, there's a group licensing arrangement that kicks in allowing NBA teams to use his likeness. But before a player signs, he can cut a deal with companies that make "draft-pick" trading cards. And I'm here to tell you that everybody wanted Shaq. We finally made a deal with Classic Cards, which meant that no other company could have me in their draft-pick set. Classic sold about $25 million in sets over the six-month period they had between June and December, and several other companies went out of business because they didn't have Shaq cards. We sort of knew something big was going on then.

But, obviously, from the beginning the big deal was going to be shoes. It's funny, when I was just starting to play ball, kids didn't think much about what we were playing in. High-priced sneakers and all the endorsement wars were just starting when I was learning to play, and I never had the money to get all excited about it. I just basically took what my dad could afford and lots of times it was those old Chuck Taylor Converses. One year in college it was a big deal when we switched from Converse to LA Gear because Coach Brown got a contract with them and everybody asked me what I thought. "To me, a sneaker is a sneaker," I always said. By the time I was ready to go pro, though, a sneaker was most definitely more than a sneaker. It was financial security.

Leonard sent out letters to a bunch of shoe companies right after he signed on as my agent. But, really, we thought all along that there were only two that had the contract money, the prestige, and the marketing dollars to sign me—Reebok and Nike. There were companies like Fila that would come up with the money but just didn't have the marketing. And then there was Asics, which probably had the money and the marketing. But I didn't feel like getting on a plane and flying all the way to Japan to talk to them.

We took the trip to Reebok first in May 1992. When we got to their headquarters, which is located in suburban Boston, every employee in the place was standing in the lobby wearing a T-shirt that said WHO'S THE MAN? on the front and on the back it said SHAQ. Everybody was cheering and waving and seemed to be real happy to see me. As I said before, I'm not the kind of guy who gets impressed easily, but I gotta say this impressed me. They really made me feel that I *was* the man, and, really, that's the main reason I ultimately went there. They gave me my own specially made jacket, too, and that turned out to be a better move than they ever thought since I wore it to Nike the following week.

Anyway, the Reebok people took us up to a meeting room with their ad agency and showed us the story boards and even sample footage for a couple Shaq commercials they had already made up. They hadn't signed up Wilt Chamberlain and the other legends yet, but they had the basic idea down. The one thing they didn't have ready was a Shaq sneaker. That would come later, they said, and I could help design it. I liked that idea. I got introduced to everyone, right up to the chairman and CEO, Paul Fireman. In another room, meanwhile, they went to work on Leonard's head, trying to get him to sign a deal right there and then for a joke amount of money, maybe one-fourth of what we eventually signed for, and telling him that the deal wouldn't be on the table very long. But Leonard held out.

"We made a promise to visit Nike," he told them, "and we're gonna keep it."

So the next week, Leonard, my father, and I flew out to Beaverton, Oregon, home of Nike. They didn't have a band or any kind of welcoming committee, but, as I said, I welcomed them with my Reebok jacket. Leonard wasn't too happy with me, but sometimes I just get frisky. We talked to all the top people at Nike, right up to Phil Knight, the president. It was funny, Phil paid no attention to the jacket, never made a comment about it, and didn't even seem to notice. But about an hour into our visit, Andre Hawkins, one of the Nike guys, pulled Leonard aside and said, "Listen, man, you're driving Phil crazy with that Reebok jacket. Can't I get you some Nike things?" But I kept wearing it. Once in a while you gotta see 'em sweat.

Nike's presentation wasn't so much Shaq-related as it was Nike-related. Their attitude was kind of "We're Nike and you should be honored and privileged to be with us, and while you're at it, it wouldn't be a bad idea if you kissed the ground when you went out the door." They did have a shoe specially made for me, a real nice-looking one with a strap up the back. But they didn't want to put my name on it and just wanted to call it Air Attack Force. They told me: "We're gonna put your name on it along with Barkley and some others." That's the phrase that stuck with me—"along with."

Instead of bringing out a dollar offer at the end of the afternoon, they got us around the table and said, "Look, when it's time to showcase you we'll do it better than anyone. You just have to tell us if you want to be with Nike and tell us what it would take." None of us liked that approach, especially my dad, who basically went nuts. That's not the way you negotiate. We wanted to hear, "Shaq, we want you," and they wanted to hear, "Nike, Shaq wants you." That evening, we went out to dinner with their top people, Phil Knight included.

We had a really nice time: me, my mom and dad, Phil Knight, Richard Donahue (the president), Tom Clarke (v.p.), Fred Schreyer, Howard White, and Leonard. However, at the end of the evening, Richard Donahue got up and said, "I want to make a toast. I want to thank everyone for attending. It's been a great evening, but the real question is: Shaq, do you really want to be with Nike?" I saw Leonard cringe, then I looked at my dad, and his neck was bulging—but somehow he managed to keep his composure. Although none of us said a word, at that moment we all knew in our hearts that the answer to Donahue's question was no.

Later, some people reported that Nike passed on me, or that they only talked to me to drive up the price for Reebok. I don't think that's true. They're business people and if they weren't interested in me they wouldn't have had us out there. But I just didn't want to beg to be there. They have a great product, but I don't want to be lined up behind Jordan, Barkley, and David Robinson. They told me I wouldn't even be able to do a commercial until I proved myself, whereas Reebok was saying, "You're The Man. We'll give you your own line. We'll let you do two commercials." By the time I left Oregon, I knew that I'd be going to Reebok.

When Leonard got back to L.A. after the Nike visit, he got a call from Mark Holtzman, Reebok's director of promotions, asking him to fly back east immediately and sign the deal. Okay, Leonard said, but here are the terms: a certain amount guaranteed minimum per year for five years, just for shoes, and Paul Fireman, Reebok's chairman, had to be available to finalize the deal. Holtzman called right back and said, "When can you be here?" Leonard flew to Boston that next morning and he and Fireman closed the deal. I think the best thing about my contract is that it required Reebok to start a separate Shaq division of the company. I get a big guarantee, royalties on every article of shoes and clothes sold, and all the advertising I do for Reebok goes to support the new Shaq division. Also, I have enough stock options at a price of $22 (well below the market price) to give me a fair stake in the company.

Just as important, Reebok agreed to commit $50 million in advertisement and promotion over the first couple years of the deal. That's a lot of money, but you gotta remember how the sneaker business works. It's what they call the "signature endorser" who really makes a shoe company. Nike was successful, but it was Jordan, and maybe Bo Jackson, who made them *really* successful. That's what I hope to do for Reebok. Mr. Fireman says that he wants to pass Nike as the number one shoe company before 1996. Players like Shawn Kemp, Danny Manning, Dennis Rodman, and myself are going to take them there. Don't look back, Nike—we're coming to get ya.

● ● ●

Soon after the Reebok deal got done, I was drafted by the Magic and that meant Leonard had to get busy on my contract. Of course we started out with a high number, around $70 million for ten years, because that's what you do when you negotiate. The figure we landed up with, around $41 million for seven years, just sounded right to all of us. When I was in college, Rick Majerus, the University of Utah coach, said I could be "the world's first $100 million player." So I'm underpaid. I'm taken care of for the rest of my life if I do the right things. I don't have any crazy clauses in my contract that say I have to be the highest paid player, king of the earth, or president of some South American country. That's the one thing I don't like about athletes—they always try to outdo each other. If one baseball player gets $5 million, another one wants $7 million. I don't think like that.

For example, if Chris Webber or Jamal Mashburn come into the league this year and get $44 million for seven years, I'll say, "Congratulations, take care of your family, enjoy yourself, bro." Because even though they may be making a little more than me, we all have the same things. Houses, cars, clothes. What's the difference when everybody has enough to make them happy?

Besides, there's a trend we must follow here. Ewing came out, made a lot of money, but Robinson came out and made more. And I made more than him. We must keep going up. Some guys who aren't as good as me are going to get paid more, but that's just life. I refuse to be one of those guys who starts complaining the minute somebody makes more money.

Now, I'm sure there's a lot of people who look at my Magic contract and think, "Wow! No basketball player is worth $5 million per year." And they're probably right. At the same time, I don't recall putting on no Lone Ranger mask and walking into Pat Williams's office with a six-shooter. Players are paid what they're paid because teams think they're worth it. Period. And lots of times it's the teams that get the best deal. In my rookie year I made about $3 million because the contract was structured to pay more on the back end, about $8.4 million in the final year. Who knows? That $8.4 may look like a bargain in 1999. The Bulls pay Jordan about $4 million per year. They could pay him $20 million and it wouldn't be enough. Sports salaries are all relative, too. Someday, players in the 21st century will be laughing at ol' Shaq. *Man, he only got $40 million for seven? What was the matter with that brother?* Back when Pat Williams was general manager of the 76ers everybody went crazy when he wanted to pay $3 million to buy out this one player's contract, and also pay the player $3 million over six years. That player was Dr. J. and Pat Williams had himself a bargain.

Anyway, the contract negotiations between the Magic and Team Shaq were about as smooth as these things can go in this day and age. No cussin' or name-calling in the newspapers, no fake threats and pretending I was gonna play in Europe or someplace where I don't even like the food. From the beginning Leonard and I made it clear that we didn't want to drag things out and make it tough on my new employer. And they've said many times in public how easy we made it. In fact, people later told me that no No. 1 pick had signed so quickly since Mark Aguirre with the Dallas Mavericks back in 1981.

We knew the Magic was really under a time crunch to get it done because, right at the start of our negotiations, the Mavericks signed Stanley Roberts to an offer sheet for a lot of money. That meant the Magic had to match the offer or lose Roberts and get nothing in return. And because of the way the salary cap worked, they had to get my contract done before they matched the offer on Stanley. That meant within two weeks. No big-money contract has ever been done in that brief period of time.

Sound complicated? It was, especially since they eventually traded Stanley, which I'll tell you about later. Plus, with what they were going to have to pay me, they had to convince several of their established players to accept restructured contracts. I didn't feel real good about that, but I didn't feel real bad, either. That's life in the NBA. Every time a high draft pick is signed, his team has to do certain things to maneuver around the salary cap. That's reality. Funny things happen all the time with contracts, a lot funnier than Shaq getting $40 million over seven. Terry Catledge, for example, has a six-year deal, and that doesn't look too good for either Terry or the Magic. He spent last season on the injured list and, right now, it looks like he'd be happier somewhere else.

One thing Leonard negotiated into the contract was a window for me to get out after four years. That's not being selfish. Again, that's reality. At this point, I can't imagine playing anywhere else but Orlando. I want to stay here, I want to win a championship here. But funny things happen. Teams change their mind about players and players change their mind about teams. Look what happened with Charles Barkley in Philadelphia. He was far and away their best player, but, eventually, he couldn't stand the Sixers and they couldn't stand him. That isn't going to happen to the Magic and me, but it's good business sense to be able to think things over again after four years.

I actually signed my contract in secret on August 5, two days before the official ceremony and press conference, in a suite of rooms in the Omni Hotel right across the street from Orlando Arena. Nobody knew about it except the Magic and my family. All seven copies of the contract were right there, stacked up on the piano. My mom had to sign, too, because I was a minor at the time, only twenty years old. I couldn't sign my contract officially, I couldn't take a drink in public, and in some states I couldn't even vote. But I could make $40 million.

Great country, huh?

And I'll tell you what the best thing about it was—I now had the money to go out and really thank the people who had done the most for me. One day I drove a black Mercedes up to my dad's house, left the keys, and said, "It's yours, bro." To be able to do stuff like that for the ones you love is the best thing about having money.

After signing the contract, I went back to San Antonio and decided I had to celebrate. Since I'm not the type of guy to throw a black-tie dinner, I went to Splashtown, a water park in San Antonio. It was real hot that day and I couldn't think of anything better. There was a dude named Uzi, a dude named Ron, a dude named Paco, a dude named Coleman, all my homeboys from San Antonio, and me. We went to the water park late in the afternoon and the guy was closing it a couple hours later. I offered him $3,000 to keep it open just for us but he wouldn't do it. See that? Money can't buy everything.

Once my name was on the Magic dotted line, I began for the first time to really feel a part of Orlando. People assume that just because a team pays you a lot of money, you automatically feel like you're a part of the city. That's not the way it works. But I'm an army brat, and, as I said before, army brats adapt pretty easily to new situations.

One of the things I knew right away was that I'd be living with Dennis Tracey, my best friend from college. We lived together during my last semester at LSU because Coach Brown let me move out of the dorm and into Dennis's two-bedroom apartment. In fact, when I was at LSU I had a marketing class in which I had to set up my own company as a project, and I made Dennis my second-in-command. Leonard thought it was a good idea when I told him I wanted Dennis to be on Team Shaq. When Leonard managed Kareem, he had an assistant, Loren Pullman, who handled a lot of his personal stuff, and it turned out to be a good arrangement. Before we got settled in Orlando, Dennis spent a couple weeks with Leonard out in L.A. learning about the business, dealing with the press, phone calls, all that stuff. Dennis had a job at the time working for a sports marketing company in Baton Rouge, but I like to tell him that I saved him from a life of poverty.

It's hard to say why Dennis and I get along so well. He's white, I'm black. He's a born-and-bred Cajun from Louisiana, I'm from New Jersey. I'm tall, he's average-sized. I'm good-looking, he's . . . Well, who can explain friendship? Dennis was one of the last walk-on guys to make LSU's program. Before he came to LSU he even wrote Dale Brown a six-page letter asking for a tryout. Dale gave him one, and eventually Dennis got a scholarship. He played one year before I came and one year with me, but had his career cut short by knee injuries. One thing I liked about him was his intensity and intelligence about the game. When we'd be choosing up sides for pickup games in Baton Rouge, I'd always take the white dude with all the kneepads on, sort of like Wesley Snipes chose Woody Harrelson in "White Men Can't Jump." And we never lost. I mean never. That's because Dennis knew what to do with the ball—throw it to Shaq.

And now he knows what to do with the phone, too—pick it up and say that Shaq's not here.

The Magic hooked us up with a realtor who had helped some of the other players, and I left a lot of the house-hunting up to my mother. The one thing I knew was that I didn't want to buy a castle; I figured I'd wait until I was king to do that. At first I thought about having a house built, but I'm not the kind of guy who likes to wait for things. I would've been out at the site every day with a stopwatch hollering at the foreman and saying, "Let's get movin, Homes." I almost moved into a high-rise condominium in downtown Orlando called the Renaissance, but they were asking $800,000. Then my mom spotted the house at Isleworth. It was $700,000 for a lot of house with real good security, so it was a much better deal. I knew as soon as I saw it that I'd take it. For me, it wasn't much more than buying a pair of shoes. Looks good. Fits good. I'll take 'em. Thanks, mom.

Dennis and I moved in pretty quickly because neither of us owned a lot of stuff. And our lifestyle right away became what I'd call "college casual." I remember hearing all these stories about how Jordan cooked and sewed for himself when he was a rookie, and to that I say, "Right on, Mike, but I'm not with you." I did little chores around the house when I was growing up, like taking out the garbage and washing dishes and even cleaning up the bathroom once in a while, but my mother never made me sweep or mop or anything like that. I grew up with four women around me, so I never had to really take care of myself. I admit that I'm kind of spoiled.

One thing I always had to do was rake the leaves that fell down from this one tree in our yard in San Antonio. My dad was a nut about that. I'd rake them into a nice pile, do a perfect job, and then I'd go down to the playground, shoot around a little bit, and come home to find the lawn loaded with leaves again. And my dad, being an army dude, would be standing there with the rake. One day I got so mad that I took an axe and started chopping down the tree, which I considered a good solution to the raking thing. My dad disagreed.

Dennis isn't any more domestic than I am, so we hired a housekeeper right away. She comes in at least two times a week, Tuesdays and Thursdays, and sometimes more often when we call her. I'm not a real sloppy guy, but I'm no neat freak, either. Sometimes when I come in I don't feel like hanging up my stuff so I just put it on the floor. When she comes in she washes my clothes, takes my stuff to the cleaner, picks up after me.

Dennis and I ain't no prize-winning chefs, either, though our timing on the microwave is perfect. We always say that we've got a lot of people who cook for us. A dude named McDonald, another one with the last name of King, a lady named Wendy, and even a guy who used to be a colonel in the army. The best thing is when my mom visits and makes me my favorite fried chicken and macaroni and cheese.

We have our games and toys, too. Right after I signed with Kenner they sent over boxes of stuff, water guns, footballs, whistles. I have two arcade type video games in there, too, one of them the NBA Video Game. It's got two players on the team, Scott Skiles and me. I always pick the Magic. Then I have Scott do the dunking and I take all the three-pointers.

I knew right away Orlando would be a nice city. Yeah, I could've made my way around L.A. without any trouble but maybe it was better to get my start in a smaller place, a place where you can feel comfortable and not get swallowed up. There's only one thing I don't like about Orlando—too many tolls on the interstates. I just hate reaching into my pocket when I'm driving and I don't carry much cash on me anyway. One day right after we moved in I called Dennis on the cellular phone from my car.

"Guess where I'm at and guess what I'm doing," I said.

"I don't know," he said.

"I'm at the toll booth writing a check for twenty-five cents," I said.

One thing I'll always remember about moving in was going shopping for stereo equipment with my mother along. I looked around for a while and finally picked out some nice stuff. Yeah, it cost a couple of thousand dollars, but I know guys who make $20,000 a year who pay just as much for their sounds. And my mom is looking this stuff over and finally she says, "Shaquille, can you put this on layaway?"

I'm moving into a $700,000 house with a $40 million salary and my mom's talking about layaway.

● ● ●

One big piece of business remained before training camp—
filming the Reebok commercials. We were supposed to do
them in the middle of the summer, but trying to get guys like
Wilt, Bill Russell, Kareem, Bill Walton, and John Wooden
together was complicated. Getting Shaq was easy. They had
me locked up when I signed with them.

The timing really couldn't have been worse. They wanted to
spend a week filming at the beginning of October, which was
exactly when I had to report to the Magic. I don't think Matty
Goukas, the Magic coach, would've exactly dug it if I called up
from L.A. and said, "Yo, I'll be there when I'm there. Later."
So we told Reebok we had to get it done in three days.

Paul Fireman sent his private plane to pick me up in L.A. and
we flew right to Las Vegas, where the first part of the legends
commercial, the part that just shows me alone shooting in a
gym, was filmed. I worked sixteen hours in one day to get it
done. Then I flew back to L.A. and worked two straight six-
teen-hour days with the legends and we were finished. Plus,
the rapping you hear in the back of the commercial? That's
me, too. I'd finish shooting, then go right to the recording
studio to lay down the rap track. By the time the whole thing
was done, I was convinced I had earned my money even if I
didn't do anything else. It's tough work being a child superstar, bro. Tough, tough work.

The commercials got a lot of attention when they finally
aired, especially my line in the beginning: "Don't fake the
funk on a nasty dunk." (My guess is you've heard it by
now.) It wasn't written originally that way by Charles Hall,
the advertising guy who came up with the concept. The first
version was, "Speak softly and carry a big stick." I didn't
like that. Anybody who knows me knows I don't talk like
that. I thought it was wack, my word for corny, silly, un-
cool. Then they wanted me to say, "Speak softly and carry
a big game." Also very wack. So, in a flash, I just came up
with the funk line. They didn't like it at first, but then it
started to grow on everybody because they realized it was

me, something I would say. Maybe one day I'll take up scriptwriting.

The commercial took a lot of work to get done. The legends had it easy for the most part, sitting over there with their arms folded or handing me the dustpan. It was a pain in the neck, having to say the same thing over and over a million times. For the first commercial, they had me dunk and dunk and dunk just to line up the shot. Then they brought in a rigged backboard, and I had to jump, press a button on the rim, then duck out of the way when it exploded. It was hooked up to a charge and it went off—PEAUGHHH!—when I hit the button. I did four of them and there was no end in sight, so I said, "Look, this is the last one." That was real glass we were dealing with, not some candy-ass stuff, and I was starting to get worried about my eyes.

Everything else—walking in the door, finding the right spot on the floor, smiling at the legends when I hold out the torn-off rim—felt comfortable to me. Later, they told me I was a natural. I hadn't done any acting before unless you count the time in first grade that I played a tree in an Easter play. (My mom says I was real good, but all I remember was having to wear this silly paper tree costume.) Plus, when I was growing up, I was horrible speaking in public, to teachers, to principals, to reporters. I used to have a stuttering problem when I was young and said "um" and "ah" a lot just to get my thoughts together. The other thing I did was make a silly face when I'd get stuck on a word and people used to laugh at me. It still takes all my concentration once in a while not to get hooked on certain words or make that face. But with practice comes experience, and I feel pretty comfortable talking in front of the cameras now. I don't want to start making speeches or anything like that, but in commercials or movies when I can play a character pretty close to myself, I'm gonna be tough to beat.

The other commercial, the one that includes the poem "If" by Rudyard Kipling, is the one with my father in it. Originally John Wooden was going to say the line at the end: "And then you'll be a man, my son." But I wondered why my own father couldn't say it. They agreed and, next thing you know, my dad was a commercial star, too. If Larry Johnson can have his grandmother in his Converse commercial, then I can have my dad in my Reebok commercial. (Wait a minute, that's not really his grandmother?) It took Dad a while, even just for that one line. Like I said before, he's from the old school, a former drill sergeant, so every time he talks it comes out as a yell. Anybody who doesn't know him assumes that he's mean. He'd be more comfortable if he was yelling the line, but eventually he got it down and it came out real fine.

After the commercials came out, everybody and his brother wanted to know how I got along with the legends. There was this real fascination with it, like we were suddenly old home-boys who were going to hang out. It was okay. I met them, I respected them, they respected me, we shook hands, and went on our way. It was a job.

The only one I really knew before the shoot was Bill Walton, who came down to LSU when I was in college and showed me some moves. I had seen Wilt around but had never really talked to him. I had met John Wooden before, when he saw me at the McDonald's High School All-America game and he had said some nice things about me. Mostly they sat around and talked about old war stories and Bill Russell did a lot of that cackle-laugh he does. "I dunked on your head, I blocked your shot, y'all used to triple-team me." Stuff like that. It was all right. Look, I'm not being smart or anything, but these guys are old enough to be my father, even Kareem, who only retired a few years ago.

Everybody seemed to be most interested in talking about Wilt because I guess I reminded people of him a little bit. That doesn't matter to me because the only person I remind myself of is Shaquille O'Neal. But if I heard it once, I heard it a thousand times: Did you know Wilt once scored 100 points in a game and got 55 rebounds and averaged 51 points over a season and . . . ? Well, I know it now. I never saw him but I'm sure he was a great player. But back in his day, Wilt was about the only 'footer in the league. And when you're seven feet tall and everyone else is lower, then you *should* average 50. These days, there's a lot of Wilts, a lot of Bills. Almost every team has one or two. The game has changed.

Don't get me wrong—100 points in a game is awesome. I know I couldn't get it today and maybe the only guy who could is Jordan. If Jordan is on, and all his shots are falling, and he's looking for 100, I guess he could get it. Later in the season, in Chicago, he had 64 against us and took 49 shots and missed a lot of them. But even that's not that close to 100. The most points I ever had in a game was 53, against Arkansas State, when I was at LSU. I could've had a lot more but probably not 100. In high school, though, I might've done it. I know I could've averaged 70 points a game because there was no one near my size or my ability. But it wasn't worth it, and my coach wouldn't have let me do it anyway. In my senior year we used to be ahead of teams like 70–12 by the end of the first half and I spent a lot of time on the bench.

When the commercials were over I think Reebok was pretty happy. The last big commercial they did, as you remember, was Dan and Dave. They should call it The Dan and Dave Disaster. Dan didn't even make it to the Olympics, Dave finished third, and the guy who won the gold medal, some Czech dude named Robert Zmelik, was wearing Reeboks and they hadn't even promoted him. Sad.

After I finished the commercials, I flew right to Orlando to begin training camp. I might've been tired and I might've been a little out of basketball shape, but I was ready.

CHAPTER FIVE

Learning the Ropes

Your ball. Your court. Your game.
      I tried to keep my father's motto in my mind but something else kept pushing itself in. Nerves.

Now, I'm always a little bit nervous before basketball games. Any player who isn't shouldn't be playing. But usually it's just kind of a slight anxiety to get it going. But on this day—October 16, 1992, an hour before my first NBA game—it was more than anxiety.

I was sitting in the locker room in Miami Arena with butterflies as big as buzzards. I couldn't explain it, but for some reason I was saying to myself: "Shaq, you're in the league now. What if you don't do good? What if you're a flop?" I don't know why those thoughts came into my head. No one had said anything about it and I hadn't read anything about it, and I never had those kinds of doubts before. But I was obsessed with the thought of, "What if I go in and I don't do no good?"

Being the number one pick doesn't guarantee that you'll be a success. I knew that. A few years earlier the Sacramento Kings took Pervis Ellison first in the draft and he never did pan out, even after he got traded to Washington. People were always waiting for "the next great center," which now I was supposed to be, and some of them hadn't lived up to expectations. Ralph Sampson was a guy I heard a lot about when I was growing up but he had only a few good seasons with the Houston Rockets. Tito Horford was a center who supposedly had athletic ability and size like me but his problem was that he didn't really have a game. And another big center, Chris Washburn, had gotten himself into trouble with drugs. I didn't compare those guys with myself, understand, but I knew that there had been flops before me, and there would be flops after me.

Secretly, see, I think a lot of people like flops. Gives them something to talk about. There would've been a lot of people real happy if I had fallen on my butt.

I wouldn't include the Orlando Magic executives among them.

It's hard to decide what fans and NBA people thought I'd be. Obviously, I was getting a lot of attention, and some were even calling me the next Wilt Chamberlain, which, as I said before, I really didn't like. But there were others who thought I'd be a flop because my college career hadn't been what some people thought it should've been. My statistics never knocked people out, and, when people look at a basketball player, they always look at numbers, because numbers are easy.

When I was a freshman at LSU I averaged only 13.9 points per game. But you gotta remember who I was playing with. Chris Jackson, who's a good player now with the Denver Nuggets, never met a shot he didn't like, and Stanley Roberts took most of the shots inside. My role was to be a rebounder and shot-blocker and that's what I paid attention to, so people thought that's what I'd be throughout my whole college career.

When I was a sophomore, Chris was in the NBA and Stanley was over in Europe, eating paella (lots of it) and playing with Real Madrid of the Spanish League. Then I started scoring like there was no tomorrow, hitting hooks, dunks, turnarounds, this and that. I averaged 27.6 points per game, almost doubling what I had done the year before which is real rare. And now people were surprised. But I wasn't. I had broken every scoring record they ever had in San Antonio when I was in high school, so it didn't surprise me.

But now people expected me to come back and double that total, maybe average 50 points a game. But I went down to 24.1 points and a lot of people called me a disappointment. You know what happened. On every play I got double-teamed, triple-teamed, quadruple-teamed, fouled, hacked, handcuffed, and assaulted, the very things that drove me out of college basketball. So people said, "This guy isn't going to be an offensive player in the NBA. He's going to be a project."

I'll show you a project, bro.

But I couldn't help it. I couldn't get their doubts out of my mind. I knew this was going to be the toughest challenge I ever faced.

● ● ●

A couple weeks before that first game in Miami, I arrived in Orlando eager to get going but a little tired and out of shape and I knew it. All my commitments over the last part of the summer had really taken away my conditioning, and I knew training camp was going to be tough. I knew it when I got in at about two o'clock in the morning and five hours later had to run the Magic's traditional twelve-minute run at some high school track.

Many of the Magic players had been working out together

since Labor Day, doing aerobics, conditioning drills, fundamentals, that kind of thing. The idea is to get into shape so you
don't have to use training camp to run yourself into shape. I
had come over when I could, but I had been in and out of
Orlando all summer and couldn't get there consistently. Fortunately, I have the kind of body that never gets real out of
shape, and I never let myself go completely.

But the run was hard. They say it was something that the
Magic copied from Dolphins' coach Don Shula, which figures,
because football coaches can be real mean guys. Everybody
runs for twelve minutes in groups according to position, and
each position has a certain distance they have to cover in those
twelve minutes. If you don't, you do it the next day. For
centers, we had to cover a distance equal to running at a
seven-minute pace for one mile. I don't know how far that was
exactly, but I know I made it, and I know it wasn't easy. If you
don't think running a seven-minute mile plus five more minutes at my size is tough, then try filling up a wagon with three
hundred pounds of bricks and lugging it around a track about
eight times. But I made it, huffin and puffin like a big ol'
locomotive and not everybody did. In fact, my pace was
about 6:45. In the process, though, I pulled my groin a little
bit, and naturally I didn't want to tell anybody about it. It
bothered me for a couple weeks, especially when we were
running suicide drills, but I didn't want to begin my career as
a guy who reported every nagging injury.

The run does prove that appearances are deceiving. In my
group, Greg Kite, who's been around the league a few years,
doesn't look like a track star but he's in pretty good shape. And
the guy in the best shape was probably Scott Skiles, who looks
like an old dude but who blew everybody away. Jeff Turner
was pretty good, too.

I felt pretty comfortable from the beginning of camp be-
cause I knew some of the players. I had played against Dennis
Scott of Georgia Tech in college and another rookie, Litterial
Green from Georgia, was in my conference, the SEC. I knew

Donald Royal from back home because he had played with the Spurs in the 1991–1992 season. I used to go watch him play and we'd be at the same clubs once in a while. I knew Jerry "Ice" Reynolds because he had been an LSU guy before I got there. I knew Brian Williams from Arizona a little. And Nick Anderson and I had built a friendship a couple years earlier when the Playboy All-American thing was held in Chicago where he's from. Nick picked me up, took me out, took me to his home.

From almost the first day my closest friend on the team, my main man, became Dennis Scott. We didn't get to know each other in college, the way Litterial and I did, and I didn't even like Dennis that much. Maybe it was because he seemed like an ACC type. But when I first got to Orlando it was Dennis who took it upon himself to show me around, tell me where to go and who to talk to, and, just as important, tell me where *not* to go and who *not* to talk to. Any professional athlete has all kinds of people coming at him from all kinds of directions, and it takes a while to sort it out. Dennis helped me do that.

For example, a guy came up to me shortly after I got to Orlando and said, "Shaq, I'm involved with underprivileged kids in the community. I like to drive them around to places, show them things."

"That sounds nice," I said.

"Yeah, and I was wondering if you'd buy me a van so I could do that," he said.

There were also all sorts of guys around who are involved with drugs and bookies. They don't wear a sign around their neck saying I'M A BAD GUY—DON'T TOUCH, so you need a person to help you. Dennis was the older brother I never had, someone to talk to and trust. We share our thoughts on women, life and especially music. Dennis is a talented dancer and rapper, two things I know a little bit about, and, as the season went on, our act became pretty well known. Finally, I think we hit it off well because we're the same kind of people. We're both real. It's all about being real. Dennis hasn't had it easy in the NBA. He struggles with his weight a little and once had to spend some time at the Duke University Diet and Fitness Center before camp. Plus, he had played in only fourteen games in the 1991–1992 season because of some complicated muscle injury called "IT band friction syndrome." Basically, the dude's leg hurt real bad. Sure, part of the reason the Magic had a bad season before I came was problems at the center position, but not having Dennis to drain those long three-point rainbows was a big factor, too.

I didn't know at all what to expect from camp when it began officially on October 9 at Stetson University. But, once it started, the funny thing was that it wasn't much different from any other preseason basketball experience. Drills, fundamentals, running. It reminded me of high school, in fact, but it was even a little easier training-wise. In high school we'd be running before practice, get a water break, then run again, then run some more. I hated it, but I think it helped me. We ran in college, too, but not nearly as much as high school.

Matty Goukas put me in the starting lineup right away and that's where I stayed. I guess they didn't even think about doing a rookie thing on me, saying that I had to "earn" the position. Orlando had won only twenty-one games the year before, so I guess nobody was pretending that changes didn't have to be made.

One of the big ones had already been made, in fact—trading Stanley Roberts to the Clippers. I found out later that there were some people in the organization fired up about the twin tower idea, but the coaches never really wanted it. They liked Stanley and all, but we're both back-to-the-basket centers, and there was no way I was coming in here and letting Stanley Roberts beat me out of a job. I feel that Stan is a good player, but sometimes he's just not motivated. You have to make Stan mad to make him be dominant. But he's going to turn out all right in the NBA. It just wasn't destined to be in Orlando. In my opinion, twin towers, especially if they're both scorers, don't work because there just aren't enough basketballs to go around. A team needs a good point guard, a good shooting forward, a big strong center, a leader, and a superstar.

One of the things the Magic did was bring in Mark McNamara, a veteran center who had never really made it big, to work with me. Mark had played with Moses Malone, Kareem, and David Robinson during his career. From the beginning it was kind of understood that Mark probably wouldn't make the team unless Greg Kite or I got hit by a bus or something. And, in fact, he didn't make it. It was a job for him, something like a temporary coach, and I felt grateful. He really, really helped me. In fact, he helped me so much that I'm not gonna tell you exactly what he said. I can't give away all my secrets now, can I, bro? But it was basically real simple stuff, like how to keep a man off balance, stuff like that. When he was done schoolin' me, he said some really nice things, like how I had the tools and the attitude to be as good as anybody. Thanks, Mark, I'll remember you in my will.

On the first day of camp at Stetson University, I was able to pretty much dominate in our first scrimmage. I made 15 out of 19 shots for 34 points. The only reason I remember the number is because they kept stats. I was able to get myself into position to dunk and, eventually, a few days later, they had to replace the rims because I put so much pressure on them. (Maybe I'll make a small donation to the Stetson alumni fund sometime.) During our first scrimmage I got the ball in the middle of the floor on a fast break, dribbled downcourt, and passed off to Scott Skiles for a layup. One of the Orlando reporters was so surprised that he wrote about it the next day. Shaq Dribbles! Shaq Passes! Well, he's gonna see a lot more of that.

I really felt good after the first day, like I was part of an NBA team. I found out later that Coach Goukas couldn't always run everything he wanted the year before because Stanley was in such bad shape. Even though I wasn't in prime form, I wouldn't let that happen. I'd die first. I could see the guys were looking for me and I played well, and Dennis was saying "We're gonna be winnin' now. The big fella is here."

I don't want to pretend I understood everything about the NBA and how to play in it. But I never really felt overwhelmed. I was playing with NBA guys all summer, so I think I had a little bit of a head start. You don't go up against Magic and Hakeem without some stuff rubbing off. But there was a lot to learn. In the NBA, for example, the center has to come out to the perimeter to set a pick for the guard on the high pick-and-roll play. It took me a while to figure out the angles to set the pick from since I almost never had to do that in college. Also, NBA teams double-team you a lot of different ways. Sometimes they'll send a guy right away. Sometimes they'll wait for you to dribble. Sometimes they'll fake coming at you right away, then wait, then do the opposite thing next time down the floor. In college, it wasn't that sophisticated. Their strategy was to come at me in droves all the time, like Indians rushing a fort.

The coaches went over all the looks I have when I get double-teamed and have the ball. The first one is to see a guy diving through the middle of the lane for a layup. Usually, it's the guy who threw the pass because we don't want his defender to double-team me. But that's not usually there, so I'm supposed to look for the open guy, first on the ball side, and then on the weak side, which means the guy across the lane, away from the ball. A lot of people talked about the troubles I had getting rid of the ball when I got double-teamed, and I'll admit that was a problem. But for *any* center who gets double-teamed that's the problem. Years after they got in the league people are still talking about Hakeem and Patrick Ewing having trouble doing that. And remember this: it's only the centers who *demand* a double-team that have to worry about it.

Defensively, I had to learn how to body a guy out of the lane because, in college, what did I care if he got good post-up position on me—I was going to block his shot anyway. Also, I had to learn what to do on isolation plays. Because I'm a shot-blocker, the coaches told me that a lot of teams were going to move my man out of the action, send him away from the ball and far away from the basket. I had to learn how to stay close enough to him to be within the league's illegal defense guidelines, but also stay involved enough to be able to do what we call "drop to the rim." That means go over to help out when a player drove, maybe clog up the lane, maybe change a shot, maybe block it.

I discovered things about my own game, like, for example, that I'm better coming into the post and getting the ball on the move, rather than just standing there and posting up. Early on we put in the two plays that we ran to death all year for me—the back pick with me starting at the top of the circle, and the cross-screen on the baseline. Both of those got me the ball kind of on the move. Eventually, all teams do basically the same thing. You watch Utah, and you'll see that Karl Malone gets to the ball almost the same way every time. How many ways do you think the Chicago Bulls have to get Michael Jordan the ball? Players make plays, not the other way around. The thing you have to work on is execution and that comes with repetition and experience.

One thing I never did quite get used to, though. On the second or third day of practice, Greg Kite grabbed the back of my jersey when I was going up for a rebound, and I whirled around like I was going to hit him. He explained to me that he did it because he wanted to show me it was one of the things you can get away with. I termed those kind of things VBs, for Veteran Bumps. But some VBs I never liked and I won't do. I don't grab jerseys or put both of my arms around somebody, even though that's apparently how you're supposed to do it in the NBA. I don't like doing it and I don't like when somebody does it to me. Later on in the season the Detroit Pistons found that out.

When training camp was over, I felt good, both about myself and the team. I felt like I was an NBA player even though I had a long way to go. And I felt like we had a team. Something that Scott Skiles said stuck with me. When a reporter asked him about me, he said: "Shaq could be the biggest jerk in the world because of all the money and attention he's getting, and we couldn't do one thing about it. But he isn't."

Thank you, Scott. The trick is staying that way.

• • •

The funny thing about the exhibition season was I didn't know it existed. A few days before that first preseason game against Miami, I was talking to one of our assistant coaches, Brian Hill, about my groin, which was still kind of tight.

"You think you should rest it?" Brian asked me.

"No way," I said. "This counts."

"Whatta you mean?" Brian said. "These games don't count."

Well, you learn something new every day. We had played exhibition games in college, against the Russian team for example, and I knew they didn't count in the conference standings. But we still counted them in the season record. That's what every college team does, which is why some of them are like 113–0 before they play anybody good.

Even at that, though, I didn't want to sit out. Too excited. Too juiced. Too many people had come to see me play.

When we checked into our hotel in Miami, the Mayfair House, before that first exhibition game there was a crowd of maybe fifty fans waiting outside. I figured this was normal until someone told me, "Hey, Shaq, fans didn't follow around the Magic until you showed up." Everybody was asking for autographs and yelling my name, and I turned to Alex Martins, the Magic's publicity guy, and said, "Well, looks like I'm going to be ordering a lot of room service." That turned out to be an accurate prediction.

Next thing I knew, I was sitting in that locker room, feeling the nerves. I looked down at my jersey. Number 32. By that time a lot had been written about Shaq and the number controversy, so I might as well tell you how I felt about it.

A number is no big deal. Players make numbers, numbers

don't make players. But the only thing that bothered me was early on when I was talking to the Magic, I said, "Can I have my college number 33?" And a whole bunch of people, including Pat Williams, said, "No problem, Shaq." When I went down to Orlando for that first visit they had a Shaq 33 jersey for me. Somebody then asked me about Terry Catledge, who had worn the number in his three years with the Magic and I said, "My understanding was that Terry Catledge said it was all right."

But Terry Catledge, when it came down to it, didn't say it was all right. He didn't want to give it up, and then somehow his brother got involved in it, trying to turn it into a rookie-veteran thing. You know, "Well, the veteran player shouldn't have to give in to the rookie." That kind of thing. I didn't look at it like that. I was just told I could have the number, so I was expecting it. But when it didn't happen, I wasn't going to go tear up my contract or anything. I'm not a whiner. I'm not a crybaby. And I won't take the shirt off of no man's back. (Not even Terry Catledge.)

Actually, I had worn 32 before I wore 33. That was back for my team in Germany. I had wanted 33 but they didn't have one so I went for 32. Then, when I got to San Antonio, I chose 33 for a simple reason—that's what Kareem wore. It seemed like a center's number or maybe that was just because he turned it into a center's number. And then Ewing came along and wore 33, too, and I was more convinced than ever that it was right for me.

So, when Terry wanted to keep 33, I just hopped right on back into 32. No problem. Just because Magic Johnson made it famous for guards doesn't mean I can't make it famous for centers. Even if Terry isn't with us, I won't take back 33. I'm a 32 man now.

Well, ol' 32 finally got over his bad case of nerves and went out for his first game. And two things happened right away. First, when the ball came in to me I got double-teamed immediately. We had been talking about it all through camp but I still thought I'd have to score like six or seven buckets before they'd really do it. But, nope, it came right away. And I made some bad decisions. I finished the game with nine turnovers and the next day I went over them on tape with Brian Hill. I couldn't believe some of the mistakes I made, and, as the year went on, I made fewer and fewer of them. My main problem was trying to force the ball to the cutter because I had always been taught that if a guy cuts, give him the ball for a layup. But defenses in the NBA are so good that sometimes they have that man covered even when it seems they don't. Magic made a career out of making that pass in the split second when his teammate was open. John Stockton and Mark Price can get it there, too. I'll never be like them, but I'm not gonna forget about that pass, either. What my coaches wanted me to do was not force the difficult pass but make the easy one.

The other thing that happened right away was that Rony Seikaly, the Heat center from Syracuse, took it right to me, challenged me. That's fine. But I sent his first shot into the seats. I consider it an insult when a guy smaller than me tries to overpower me. Well, I guess I'd consider it an insult if Godzilla tried to overpower me. Then, right after that, John Salley went up for a shot and threw it over the backboard. I think he knew I was in the vicinity. Scott Skiles went up to Seikaly and said, "It's a whole new ballgame, Rony."

I finished with 25 points, hitting on 11 of 16 shots, 6 rebounds and 3 blocked shots. All in all I felt good about the way I played, except for those nine turnovers. My NBA career had begun on a high note.

I never got ridiculous expectations about it, though. I knew there would be bad games and losses, along with the good games and wins. For the rest of our exhibition season, I just concentrated on trying to learn NBA basketball and also deal with all the strange stuff that was happening to me off the court.

In our third exhibition game, for example, we played the Charlotte Hornets in Asheville, North Carolina. And as I was getting dressed before the game, I suddenly looked up and there were two fans, standing there grinning at me and asking for my autograph. They had just walked into the locker room and nobody stopped them. It was okay because they were really nice, but what if they had had a knife, like that nut case who went after Monica Seles later in the season? Gool ol' Shaq would've been good as gone. Alex Martins happened to walk in when I was talking to them and he couldn't believe it.

"What are you guys doing in here?" he said.

"Oh, we're just talking to Shaq," they said.

He threw them out and talked to the arena officials about better security after the game. So when we left there were about one thousand fans outside who basically bowled over the two security men following us. We had to fight our way to the bus. I can still see Lenny Currier, our trainer, leading the way, jacket half off, his slicked-backed hair all disheveled, looking like some pulling guard in the NFL. I'm not saying every fan was there just to see me, but it seemed like a lot of them were calling my name. I started to wonder if my teammates were glad I was around or not.

We lost the game 117–112. I had been looking forward to going against Alonzo Mourning, who was picked right behind me in the draft, but he was still sitting out because of a contract dispute, exactly what I had wanted to avoid. But Larry Johnson was playing and he really grabbed my mind. Strong, fast, agile, tough, can play. I knew him pretty well from our games against UNLV in college, and I love his commercials where he plays his own grandmama. They're good because they show his personality. He's a ham, a funny, crazy, likable guy, and that's what comes through. That's why I think people like my commercials, too, because they're true to my personality.

We lost our fourth exhibition game, 108–98, against Minnesota in Orlando, basically because we couldn't make an outside shot to save our life. For some reason my knees felt real bad during that game. I have a throwback once in a while to when I was young and battling Osgood-Schlatter's. But in the

NBA you don't have any choice but to suck it up. When they start hurting so bad that I can't put the pain to the back of my mind, it'll be time to get out. That won't happen for at least another two years. Just kidding, Pat Williams.

I had 19 points, and Christian Laettner, the third pick in the draft, had 25 for the Timberwolves. Everybody expects me to say bad things about Christian. He beat me out for player of the year in college and he was chosen ahead of me (and Alonzo and Jimmy Jackson and a lot of other guys) to be the one college player on the Dream Team. But I'm not going to say bad things.

I'll admit that I was a little disappointed when I wasn't college player of the year. It seemed like I got most of the press, was on the cover of *Sports Illustrated* and all, and he got player of the year. But maybe he deserved it because of how well Duke did and how well he did in the big NCAA games. I can't take that away from him.

Christian and I went up against each other twice in college. Well, not really up against each other because we checked each other for only a few minutes. I know he can take me outside, and he knows he doesn't want to stay in my neighborhood, down by the basket, or I'll stick him bad. Anyway, the first time, which was during my sophomore year, he got me pretty good at Duke. We had to play them on a Sunday, a day after we had played against Georgia. Georgia was a game we needed in the conference and it was a real tough one. I had a triple-double—37 points, 19 rebounds, 10 blocks, in an 89–86 victory. And I was a little tired for the Duke game, a little bruised up, a little used up. I was lollygagging out there, I'll admit it. Laettner had 24, I had only 14, and the media built it up as "Laettner Beats Shaq."

But the next year when they came to LSU, we were more ready for them. We were leading by ten at one point, but they kicked it back up and landed up beating us 77–67. I outplayed Laettner this time. I had 25 points, 12 rebounds, and seven blocks. He had 22 and 10. But they won the game.

As far as the Olympic team goes, sure, I was disappointed at first. I think part of the reason he got picked ahead of me was that Christian always played on the international teams in the offseason, and I was never into that. Between my freshman and sophomore years in college, I played in the U.S. Olympic Festival in Minnesota for the South team because my college coach, Dale Brown, was the South coach and he asked me to. I'm not lying when I say I dominated. I nearly averaged a triple double and got the MVP award. When someone asked me why I played I said, "Because my coach asked me to, and you don't say no to your coach." I was telling the truth. But I turned down an invitation to play for the U.S. in the Goodwill Games in Seattle later that same summer because I just wanted to rest my body. And I didn't play for any other touring teams either. I wanted to spend time with my family, I wanted to rest, and I had to earn some money. Meanwhile, Christian and some other guys played all the time, and the selection committee didn't forget that.

Anyway, if you look back at the 1992 Olympics, they really didn't need me. They had two great centers in David and Patrick and, with the competition they were facing, either could've played with a cast on and still dominated. I'm sure Christian had a great time getting to know the players and all, but, the way I am, I would've wanted to be on the court playing, not on the bench. It sounded good, just being over there and playing with the stars, but I would've gotten itchy. And when I didn't go, it enabled me to get a lot of other things done over the summer, a lot of deals, a lot of playing with NBA guys. That's not rationalizing. That's just reality. Now that the pros are established in the Olympics, there will be other opportunities for me to represent my country if it works out.

Anyway, I don't blame Christian for any of it. Every time I see him it's like, "Hi, how you doin? How's your family?" I met his mother once and I tell him to say hi for me. I'll tell you this—Christian's gonna be a star. I don't want to say we'll be exactly like Bird and Magic because they're two of the greatest players ever. But I think there's going to be a rivalry and respect between us that's really going to be good for the NBA. There's a lot of similarities to Bird and Magic. One of us is black, outgoing personality, smiling a lot, picking up kids, petting puppies, helping old ladies across the street. The other is white, kind of inward, frowning, secretive, a little mysterious. I assume you know which is which.

Our record was 1–3 after the Minnesota game, but, just like that, we turned it right around again. That's one thing about the NBA—there's so many games you get to redeem yourself with, and I like that. One source of pride for me is not having two bad games in a row. I'm not saying it's never going to happen, but it won't happen very often. We smashed the Hornets 131–102 at home, beat the Hawks twice, once at home, once in Atlanta, then beat Minnesota 110–105 in our final exhibition game. That was played at Rapid City, South Dakota, for some reason. We played in some weird places in college, but I'll tell you, in the NBA preseason you could land up anywhere. Maybe I'll suggest playing a game in Wiesbaden, Germany, at my father's old army base next season.

Anyway, in South Dakota, somebody organized a trip to Mount Rushmore and asked if I wanted to go. I told them that maybe when they have Martin Luther King up there, too, I'll make the trip. I'm not being unpatriotic or anything, but it would just have more meaning for me if he was up there with them.

After the game, security was again real lax and a bunch of fans surrounded me, demanding autographs and one guy even ripped a strap off my coat, one of my Jeff Hamilton coats, in fact. Now, that's the kind of thing that really makes me mad but I held my temper. I could've seen the headline: "Shaq beat some dude up just because he ripped his coat."

Judging by the exhibition games, which I considered pretty successful, I could tell that the regular season was going to be interesting, both on and off the court.

And I wasn't wrong.

CHAPTER SIX

Takin' the League by Storm

I'll admit it. As a kid I dreamed about being rich. I started out in the 'hood where nobody had much of anything, and, then, when I started living on army bases, I'd see the officers' kids with their new bikes and new sneakers and I'd want what they had. My father wanted me to be rich, too, only he had a plan. One day he took me aside, shoved a basketball in my face, and said:

"You see this ball? You take care of this ball, you love this ball, you sleep with this ball, you dream with this ball. Because someday this ball is going to put food on your table."

I don't know whether my father ever dreamed it would be $40 million worth of food, but he was right.

My point is this: it all came down to playing ball. The reason

I was where I was on November 6, 1992—preparing for my first official, regular-season, count-it-in-the-standings-no-b.s.-ing-around NBA game—was ball. Nothing about my personality, or my looks, or what college I went to, or how much I was getting paid by Reebok. It was all about ball.

Personally, sitting there in the locker room before the game at Orlando Arena, I never thought about my age, which at the time was only twenty years, eight months. Even when I hung around with older kids growing up, I never felt young, partly because of my size, partly because I thought I was as smart and as aware as any of my friends. (Once I stopped being a goofball, that is.) But people were always bringing it up to me and writing about it. Pat Williams, the Magic general manager, had a couple pretty good lines about it. "He's so young we've hired a team dermatologist" was one of them. "He's so young he signs his autographs with crayon" was another. Personally, I don't do young jokes.

But even compared to other rookies, I was young, at least two years younger than most of them, including Litterial Green, who could pass for my kid brother. And when I thought about where the other great centers in the game were when they were my age, it was a little scary.

At age twenty, Wilt Chamberlain was beginning his sophomore season at the University of Kansas. Bill Russell was just finishing his first season at San Francisco and he stayed for three more after that. Bill Walton was starting his third season at UCLA. Kareem was wrapping up his second season at UCLA, and Patrick Ewing was just starting his second at Georgetown. Hakeem was in the middle of his junior season at Houston.

And me? I was getting ready to play the Miami Heat.

Just because I was young, though, people weren't afraid to heap on the pressure. I knew how much the team was counting on me, and how much my being drafted meant to the entire city. Jack Swope, the team's assistant general manager, was talking one day about how Disney and Sea World, as great as they are, can't match the excitement of actually having a real person to root for. That's why people were so interested in me. I'm flesh and blood. I could smell the excitement in the air, feel the electricity around the arena. But I tried not to get caught up in it. The pressure and the expectations went with the territory and the big contract and that's okay. But I had to play to satisfy myself and my team. Nobody else. If I happened to be entertaining in the process and turned the fans on, well, that would be great.

One thing I knew—I wanted to make the Magic a lot better team than they had been the year before. I couldn't imagine dealing with a 21–61 season like they had in 1991–1992. And I knew that if we weren't better, it would be my fault. Lots of rookies had come in and turned their teams around, like David Robinson and Larry Bird. On the other hand, the Knicks won one less game in Patrick Ewing's first season even though he was voted rookie of the year. One player shouldn't get all the credit or all the blame, but I knew that's what would happen.

I had said coming out of college that I'd average something like 14 points and 8 rebounds, and a lot of people jumped all over my case. I didn't know. I really didn't. They seemed like reasonable numbers at the time. I'm positive that Michael Jordan didn't come into the league thinking he would ring up thirty a night. And the young players who start talking about tearing up the league are exactly the ones who don't. What most rookies do is take a look at their college numbers and figure that in the NBA they're just naturally going to be a little less. That's what I did.

Obviously, by the time I was through with training camp and our exhibition season, I saw that my numbers were going to be better than I first thought. But I still didn't have a goal in mind when the season began. I think that's when you get yourself in trouble.

My father set really low standards for me as a basketball player. He wanted me to block shots like a Bill Russell, rebound and make the outlet pass like a Wes Unseld, score like a Wilt or Kareem, handle the ball like an Oscar Robertson or a Jerry West. That's all. I didn't know all those guys when he was talking about them, but I know them now, and I know it was impossible to be that kind of player in my first year. But his point was to be versatile instead of one-dimensional, to impose my will on every part of the game every minute I was on the floor. That advice I took to heart.

I'll tell you what I was thinking before my first game, and I don't want it to sound cocky. But I'm 7'1", 303 pounds, and my philosophy has been to never, ever, ever, let a man who's lighter than me or smaller than me dog me out. It's just against everything I stand for. Average players I was not going to worry about at all. Period. They might have some years over me, or they might know some things I don't, but I can compensate with my size and my natural ability and especially with my will. Once I discovered I could play in the league after my summer games and training camp, the only guys I was going to worry about were Robinson, Hakeem, Ewing, Brad Daugherty, the top centers.

My size, my body, is an asset. I'll be the first to admit it. But when you live with a body maybe you look at it a little different than everyone else. For example, I probably can't do many more than ten pushups. I can't do many situps. I could hardly do one pullup. I can't stand on my hands and walk around, like David Robinson used to do at the Naval Academy. I can bench press about 250 pounds but not like ten times, maybe just once or twice. A guy like Greg Kite would be better than me lifting weights. I have a good vertical jump for a 'footer, something like 28 or 29 inches, but it could stand improvement. And I'll tell you something else. I don't have a chest at all. I've got a bird chest for someone my size. My arms are funny, too. If I look at them when I'm not doing anything they seem all flabby. But when I look at pictures of myself when I get the ball down low, holding people off and ready to attack the basket or something, they look real big. I'm like two different people sometimes.

What I think I have is inner strength—the drive, the will, the determination to succeed. Maybe that's why my arms are all pumped up when I look at the photos. Inner strength. That's what's brought me this far, and that's what will keep on carrying me.

●　●　●

The night before that first official NBA game, I stayed up till dawn plotting strategy. I watched films of Miami center Rony Seikaly, I slept with my Orlando Magic playbook under my pillow . . . I studied . . . just kidding. Actually, what I did was stay up too late playing a video game called Sonic the Hedgehog with my four-year-old nephew, Malcolm. We had been riding around Orlando that evening and we stopped at Toys "R" Us, and I bought him whatever he wanted. It was good therapy for me, too. One of the first things I did when I got to Orlando was buy ten season tickets for my family and people like Leonard Armato so they could come down and watch any time they wanted without me having to run around for tickets.

I already know some NBA players who spend as much time being a ticket broker as being a player, and it's a huge pain. A couple of times when I was at LSU and we played a game in the New Jersey area, all my relatives who were still back there wanted tickets. I just told them to call Dad. We only got four tickets then and we had to buy them. Wherever he was, Dad was in charge of collecting the money and handing out the tickets. I didn't want no part of it. Besides, he's better at setting people straight if they didn't like their seat or couldn't get a ticket.

Before one game in college, I happened to eat a piece of pizza and some pasta a few hours before a game and I played real well that night. So I continued that routine and decided to do it in the NBA, too. Once we got settled in Orlando, I found a place that either Dennis or I would stop at or get it delivered. Two slices of pizza and a big bowl of spaghetti. I don't use the word "superstition," but I guess that's what it is. In some situations I like new experiences, but other times I like my routines. I always drive from my house to the arena the same way, for example. One day when Dennis was driving he made a different turn before I realized what was going on.

"You gotta stop and go back, bro," I said to him.

"You're kidding, right?" he said.

I wasn't. We went back and went to the arena on the Shaq Track.

Sometimes I think it's silly. Other times I don't. I didn't have my pizza and pasta lunch on March 30, and that's the night, as you'll see, that I got into a small disagreement with Bill Laimbeer and Alvin Robertson of the Detroit Pistons.

My classes at LSU usually ended by 12:30, so I'd always take a nap before a game, too. I continued that custom for home games in Orlando. I set the alarm even though Dennis would always come in to wake me up anyway. Plus, I have all the clocks set thirty minutes ahead in my house, so there's not much chance I'll oversleep. Like a lot of athletes I know, I can go to sleep right away, but I have this kind of inner alarm in my head that whispers, "Shaq, time to get up. You've got a job to do." That alarm was certainly working before my first game.

When I arrived at Orlando Arena that evening, the first thing I had to attend to was making sure the Shaq Pack went okay. Before the season began I had bought another twenty season tickets for disadvantaged kids. Alex and Dennis really helped me out, getting a list of all the kids' organizations around Orlando and picking out which games were for which groups. All the kids sat in one section. We gave them shirts, an autographed picture of me, and a Shaq basketball card, which these days is like giving away a stock certificate. Once it got rolling, an intern in the Magic office named Jeff Ryan kept it going and did a great, great job. At one point I went out and bought Jeff four suits to thank him. As long as I'm in Orlando, the Shaq Pack will continue.

There was nothing special about my pregame feelings. I was

an NBA player and it was time to go out and take care of business. The Magic did one thing different in their pregame routine. They usually announced forward, forward, center, guard, guard in the introductions, but they decided to name me last. When I ran out, Stuff, the Magic mascot, bowed down in front of me.

We also gave the home fans their first official look at The Knuckleheads. Dennis, Nick, and I all ran out with our fists at our foreheads with the knuckles up. Knuckleheads. The knucklehead thing got a lot of publicity around the league, which was funny because it was really a simple little team thing. Anyway, it got started in college with Litterial Green and me. We were friendly rivals because the competition was so hot between LSU and Georgia, and before games we used to get on each other. "Shut up, knucklehead," or, "We're gonna get you, knucklehead." I don't know why we chose that word but we did. One time the refs had us both out before the game and he said, "Okay, you knuckleheads, no rough stuff." And from then on, that was our word and we formed the group when we became teammates.

We define Knuckleheads as a bunch of guys who don't listen to anyone, who act silly, who act crazy, and who do what they want to do. Except what they do isn't warped or twisted. It's always the right thing. Make sense? Probably not. Maybe you have to actually *be* a Knucklehead to understand. On our team, Litterial and I added Dennis and Nick to the club, and, as the year went on, we added a few others, even from other teams. I'll tell you about them later.

Anyway, the Knuckleheads got it done in that first game, which we won 110–100. Knucklehead Nick had 42 points and Knucklehead Dennis had 27. It was really good to see Dennis get off like that considering the bad luck he had the year before. As for the biggest Knucklehead, well, he did all right. I came in real intense, real serious, and played solid. Twelve points, 18 rebounds, and 3 blocks. The only bad news was that I had eight more ugly turnovers. Twice I got rebounds and drove the length of the court, one time for a dunk, one time for an assist. I'm glad my high school coaches let me do that once in a while. A lot of coaches always scream at the big guy to give it up to a guard, but, once they saw I could do it, they gave me a green light as long as I didn't abuse it. I think Matty Goukas felt the same way. If I see an opportunity to take it all the way and dunk, then I'm going to do it. And, surprisingly, not many of my turnovers come in those situations. They're much more likely to come in the halfcourt offense when I'm getting double- and triple-teamed.

One thing I remember about that first game was looking up at my dad several times. He's my harshest critic and my fairest. Whenever they call a bad foul on me, we have like these airwaves, and I'll tell him in my mind, "Hey, they dogged me," and he'll say, "Don't worry about it, keep playing." Sometimes if I get the ball and go through the lane and they call a travel, I'll look at him, and he'll be nodding his head as if to say, "Yes, you traveled," and then I'll believe the call.

● ● ●

Back to backs. That's a fact of NBA life, which any young player has to get used to. (You'll notice I rarely use the word "rookie." I hate that word. I never want to hear that word again. I don't like to hear about "rookie mistakes," "rookie calls," or "the rookie wall." Why don't they call a bad pass by a ten-year player a "veteran turnover"? "Rookie" is just a word. First-year cops are rookies. First-year reporters are rookies. But I never hear the word used with them.) So, the next night after beating the Heat, there we were playing the Washington Bullets and beating them 103–96.

That was my first experience with the wacko Bullet fan, Robin Flicker, who sits behind the visiting bench and yells crazy stuff the whole game. Someone told me that for several weeks Ficker had been talking about coming after me. Maybe he even took extra yelling practice the night before the game. He was hollering stuff like, "Shaq, you're a bum, Pervis Ellison is outplaying you," or "You're not half the player Charles Jones is." Then he started in on Matty. "I remember your coach as a player, Shaq, and he stunk. Don't listen to him." And he was waving a rubber chicken around, too.

Some player will eventually strangle this dude, but I plan on paying him no mind. We won 102–98 and I had 22 points, 15 rebounds and 4 blocks. That was the best way to answer Ficker.

TNT broadcast our third game, which was back home against Charlotte, but they didn't get the Shaq-Alonzo matchup they were after because 'Zo still hadn't signed. They beat us 112–108. I had a pretty big game with 35 points, but I broke down in the fourth quarter and my shots didn't fall. That happens sometimes. After the game somebody showed me the NBA All-Star ballot that had just come out with my name spelled as "O'Neill" instead of "O'Neal." I guess they thought I'd be mad about it. I explained that I spell my name like Tatum O'Neal of *The Bad News Bears* instead of like Tip O'Neill of the United States Senate. I have a special place for Tatum because I saw in a book once that she shares my birthday. We were the only famous people listed for March 6.

We clubbed the Bullets at home 127–100 on Nov. 12 and by then people had started to notice how well we were doing. The league noticed because they made me player of the week, which was nice. It was important for me to come in and prove myself right away, prove I wasn't a bunch of seven-foot-tall hype. Wes Unseld, the Bullets' coach, noticed, too, and went off on the officials about how much I was supposedly getting away with. He said: "I don't know what the officials are seeing but I'm seeing off-hand pushing, ducking shoulders into people. You allow that and it's impossible to stop a big, strong guy."

Well, I respect Wes Unseld, who, by the way, was a "big, strong guy" himself. He was one of the players my dad told me to model myself after, the only guy ever to be named rookie of the year and MVP in the same season. But his complaining about me began kind of a trend that lasted the whole year. Sometimes I think NBA should stand for National Bitchin' Association. It seemed like half the people wanted to weigh in with their opinion on what I was getting away with, and the other half wanted to talk about "rookie calls," fouls that were called on me just because I was a rookie. I don't like talking about referees or calls or complaining about anything that I don't have control over. But because everybody talked about it so much I'm going to mention it here and try to be done with it. Or almost done with it.

I really don't think I get many breaks from the officials, and not just because I'm a rookie. I'm used to not getting calls. When I started playing I never got them because I was bigger and stronger than the other kids. I never worried about it. But I have always hated the inconsistency. If I've got four guys hammering at me and no foul is called, then fine. I can take it. But if I touch a guy at the other end and some guy does a Marlon Brando acting job and they call a foul, then that's being inconsistent.

Everybody in the league puts one hand on the guy he's guarding from time to time. Not really to hold him but just to kind of locate him. But what I heard all the time was "Stop pushing, Shaq." Well, I wasn't pushing. If I really pushed a guy, believe me, you'd see it. But a center like Rony Seikaly, when I just touch him, lay that one arm in there, he screams "Stop pushing, Shaq!" And—tweet—I get called. Consistency. It's all I ask. I don't want to be penalized for being big and strong. If I'm keeping a guy out because I'm stronger than he is, then maybe he should get in the weight room and make himself stronger. Or he should make himself quicker to get around me. But his main strategy shouldn't be to attract the referees' attention.

We played the Nets at Meadowlands Arena on November 14 and lost 124–113. I had a good game statistically with 29 points and 15 rebounds but I wasn't happy. I was trying too hard because I had so many relatives around—grandmoms, uncles, aunts, cousins, second cousins. Derrick Coleman had a good game against us, and he didn't even do much talking that night. Maybe he wasn't in a talking mood. He was later when we played them, though.

Then we went to Philadelphia to play the 76ers, and by then my routine on the road was established. Alex Martins and I had talked about how we were going to deal with all the media requests. I'm not bragging or inventing anything when I say that on my first circuit around the league every reporter in every town wanted to talk to me. It's simply the truth. So Alex and I decided that when I came into a new city I would do an individual press conference and get all the questions out of the way. We would either do it a day early if we got into town, or do it before the Magic's shootaround on the morning of the game.

I had already decided by then that I wasn't going to talk to the media right before the game. NBA locker rooms allow reporters in right up until forty-five minutes before the game and that's fine. I'll nod to them, wave to them, but I'm not going to talk to them other than to say hello. It throws off my pregame preparation if I'm yammering away to reporters. I know Michael Jordan talks before games, I know Charles Barkley talks before games. That's fine. But Patrick Ewing and a few other players don't, and that's our right.

Anyway, I considered the press conferences—all twenty-six of them, one in every visiting city—to be just part of the job. I enjoy playing basketball and for anyone who wants to play professionally there are things that come with the territory and you have to accept them. Like if someone wants to work in the post office, there are lots of things you have to do that aren't glamorous. You have to lick stamps, you have to count envelopes, you have to lift big burlap bags of mail. When I get tired of dealing with the media, it'll be time for me to do something else. Besides, when you think about it, it's not that hard. Twenty minutes talking to people is not like operating a jackhammer. But if I had turned it into a dread kind of thing—

"Aw, man, I don't feel like talking to these guys this morning"—it would've been a drag. I know some of the reason that the media seemed to like me in my first year was that I took the time to sit down and talk and didn't blow anybody off.

The hardest thing, though, was hearing the same questions over and over. Alex had to keep reminding me, "Look, you're talking to these guys for the first time. They don't know what you said in Washington a week ago." But I figured if I heard the same questions over and over, then I could give some of the same answers. I just did it with a smile and a light touch. The most popular question had to be, "Shaq, what's been the biggest adjustment?" Like I was playing with a square ball in college and now I'm playing with a round one.

But sometimes the questions weren't all that innocent. I've been dealing with the media for some time now and I understand the way some of them operate. For example, if someone asks me, "Shaq, what do you think of Alonzo Mourning?" they're really asking, "Shaq, don't you think you're twice as good as Alonzo Mourning and you're gonna dog his butt real bad?" It's not my style to say that. Even if I did believe that about any player (and I certainly don't about Alonzo) I wouldn't say it just to begin controversy. You'll see in this book that any bad things I say about a player have to do with his acting or flopping to get a foul or complaining to a referee. That's the one thing I will criticize.

We played two pretty good games in a row after that, beating the 76ers in Philadelphia 120–110 and the Golden State Warriors at home 126–102. I remember the Sixers game because Denzel Washington, who I had met in L.A. over the summer, came in to say hi. Somebody said, "Oh, the dude from *St. Elsewhere*, right?' And I said, "No, the dude who played Malcolm X." And I remember the Warrior game because that's when I slid on my belly about ten feet chasing down a loose ball, and it got replayed on ESPN about a million times over the next week. Nice slide, if I do say so myself.

One bad thing happened around this time—Brian Williams,

who had been the Magic's first draft pick the year before I came, was hospitalized for depression. He even admitted that he had attempted suicide. We just kind of left him alone to try to work things out. But it was sad. I know I can never fully understand what he was going through then. What I'm doing now could never make me sad. It was a dream for me to be playing at this level and it could never make me depressed. But they say depression is a serious illness. By the end of the season Brian was back with us and even playing real well once in a while. I hope he gets things straightened out because he has the ability to be a real good player.

And then it was time to go to New York to play the Knicks. Or, judging from the attention it was getting, it was time to go to New York for World War III. Again, it's nothing against Patrick Ewing, who is a great, great player, but I don't want to measure myself against him. And although I knew it would be a little special, I didn't want to go pretending it was a major moment in my life. It was only November, man. But I got a glimpse of what the attention would be like when a *Sports Illustrated* photographer followed me all the way from Orlando to New York, even taking photos on the team plane when I was sleeping. Every once in a while, I'd see him coming out of the corner of my eye and put a towel over my head. Gotta' make 'em sweat a little, bro.

The weekend was hectic because of all the attention the game was getting, but my dad was around a lot to keep me focused, and my mom told me something very interesting. "No matter how you do out there, Shaquille," she said, "I'll still love you." And that put it all in perspective for me. Being in New York, honestly, was nothing that special. I used to come into the city once in a while when I lived in the 'hood, but I never thought that you had to make your mark at Madison Square Garden or anything like that. And the city has way too much traffic for me to enjoy living there. It was a special place for my mom and dad, though. They both used to work for the City of Newark—my father in the violations bureau, my mother in payroll—and, after they met and started going out, they would come in to New York and walk all around Rockefeller Center and ride the escalators and look at the people, and do all the free things you did when you didn't have any money.

Of course, I had money and didn't do anything real special. My father, Leonard, and I went to dinner the night before the game. I walked around Broadway with Dennis Scott so the *SI* photographer could get his photos on Saturday morning, and, as usual, I slept in the afternoon. Over at Madison Square Garden that afternoon they were holding a women's tennis tournament, and later I found out that one of those real little players, Arantxa Sanchez Vicario, was walking around in my size 20 shoes to show how big they were. I wondered if she wanted to take my place against Patrick that night.

And then it was time to play. Well, almost. Before the game, Alex Martins asked me if I'd mind posing for a photo at midcourt with Patrick and Wilt Chamberlain, who was at the game as a fan. Yes, I did mind, and, when they threw up the ceremonial opening tip, I didn't even jump. Tell you the truth, I don't think Patrick felt much better about it than I did. But I did it as a favor to Alex because he took good care of me. It was nothing against Wilt. I was just against anything that added more to this one-on-one matchup they were trying to build between Patrick and me, and also anything that kept comparing me to Wilt. The whole thing was corny, a fake jump ball, a posed photo. But you gotta take the clouds with the sunshine, that much I know.

Patrick started quick on me. He hit a jump shot, then forced me to travel. Out of the corner of my eye I saw Spike Lee, who was sitting at courtside, almost run out on the court to make the travel sign. Chill, Spike. (Actually, I like Spike. I met him for the first time when I was in college and we talk here and there and exchange gifts when we get together. Maybe I'll make him a Magic fan before I'm through.) The Knicks are a tough team because they double-team from anywhere. Charles Oakley might come running at you from across the court, or they'll send long-armed Charles Smith, or it might be Doc Rivers, who's a big guard, coming at you from the perimeter. They probably play tougher defense than any team in the league. Also, they forced our point guard, Scott Skiles, way outside when we ran the high pick-and-roll, and he couldn't get it to me.

But then I got into it myself. I sent back one of Patrick's hooks. I spun away from him on the right side and scored. In the second quarter Oakley and I were playing real physical against each other, and they tossed him out of the game after he was hit with his second technical for throwing an elbow. I was sorry to see him go, honest. In the third period I was able to get loose for a couple monster slams, but Patrick scored some on me, too. As a team, we were never in the game. I sensed that the Knicks were playing with a lot of intensity, like they had something to prove, and we couldn't match that.

When it was over, all anyone wanted to talk about was Patrick and me and how excited we both must've been. "For some reason," I told the media, "it takes a lot to get me excited." It does, too. Somebody actually wanted to know if I could tell that Patrick was excited because of the expression on his face. Like I went to college to study facial-expression-reading. I didn't really want to talk about Patrick and me, but, when I allowed myself to study it, I thought it came out pretty even. He had 15 points, 9 rebounds, 3 blocks. I had 18 points, 17 rebounds, 3 blocks. There were a lot of times that we didn't double-team, and mostly what I remember about the night was seeing a swarm of Knick jerseys coming at me. Also, Patrick got some relief in guarding me. They had Oak and Charles Smith and even Herb Williams on me for a while.

Tell you the truth, I think there were a lot of people disappointed in the game. They either wanted to see Patrick dog me out, or they wanted to see me dog him out. But when it came out about even, nobody knew quite what to say. In the only statistic that really mattered, though, he got the best of me: Knicks 92, Magic 77.

• • •

It was funny, but right after I played against Patrick I had to go up against Hakeem, and the game didn't get one-tenth the attention. Probably because it was in Orlando. I was happy. Both of us just went out and played our game, and we won 107–94. Scott Skiles played real well with 30 points and Dennis hit four three-pointers.

Statistically, Hakeem outplayed me. He had 22 points, 13 rebounds, and 5 blocks, and I had only 12 points, 13 rebounds, and 3 blocks. The one thing I remember about the game is that I didn't get to the foul line. Not even once. (And Wes Unseld thought I was getting breaks from the refs?) Hakeem made a bunch of his shots from the outside and everyone wanted to know—and still wants to know—whether I'll have to turn myself into a jump-shooter like him to be a real success.

The answer is: I don't know. Nobody comes into the league in their first year knowing exactly what they're going to be. Michael Jordan didn't know that he'd eventually become one of the league's best perimeter shooters because, at first, he had so much success taking the ball to the hole. Magic didn't know he'd have to start shooting a little baby hook shot late in his career. Right now, jump-shooting is not my game. I want to stick with what got me here, and, once I perfect that, go to work on something else. Shooting jumpers didn't get me to this level. My role is to mix it up inside, stay low, get rebounds, dunk. I remember somebody asked Brendan Suhr, a Nets' assistant, if I could be stopped because I didn't have one pet shot. "A dunk's a pretty good pet shot," Brendan said, and I agree with that. But don't bet against me hitting those J's one of these days, bro.

The day after the Houston game was Thanksgiving, and I spent it going to two shelters downtown to serve "Shaqsgiving." Nobody told me to do it, nobody even suggested it, and I didn't do it to get attention. A couple of Orlando reporters came along only when they argued with Alex and told him that they had to cover it as a news event. Okay, fine. But that's not why I did it.

I had gotten the idea a couple weeks earlier when Dennis Scott and I were driving around. As we headed off the exit I saw a white lady standing there with a beautiful baby, half black and half white, holding a sign that said: WILL WORK FOR FOOD. It really got to me and I decided right then and there to do something even if it wasn't much.

Sure, there are times you can't tell if it's real or fake. On *60 Minutes* one time they had a story about a guy who made $90,000 on a 9-to-5 job and then spent the rest of his time in bum clothes collecting money on the streets. But you can't go through life assuming everything's a fake or pretty soon you've got nothing to smile about. As soon as I saw that little girl, I knew I'd have to do something.

I told Dennis Tracey to look into feeding the homeless on Thanksgiving. My idea was that there was maybe one hundred of them because, really, you rarely see any homeless people at all in Orlando. After Dennis made some calls, he said, "Hey, Shaq, we've really got a problem. There's more like three hundred homeless people." No problem, I told him, we'll feed all of them. So I hired a catering service and went over there myself. On Thanksgiving Day, people started lining up at 6:15 A.M.

A lot of the people had no idea who I was. They thought I was just some big black brother carving turkey and spooning up rice and peas. That was cool. It didn't make a difference to me one way or the other. I've almost been where these people were. My father worked too hard for us to be homeless, but there were times when we lived in the projects in Newark when we were on food stamps.

And when I was driving home that afternoon I turned to Alex Martins and said: What could we do for Christmas?

CHAPTER SEVEN

On the Long and Windin' Road

We finished up November with two pretty good victories, beating Indiana on the road 130–116 and the Cavaliers 95–93 at home. All in all, it was the most successful month in Magic history with eight wins and three losses. I don't think any of us thought we were going to win the championship or anything like that, but confidence was high when we took off for our first West Coast road trip.

And confidence was low by the time we got back. That's the way it goes sometimes in the NBA, bro.

Maybe it was a bad omen when it took us eight and a half hours to fly to Seattle because of strong headwinds. We even had to stop in Wichita, Kansas, to fuel up. Any time anybody starts talking about the glamorous road life in the NBA I think about trips like that.

But the team plane makes it easier. This was the first season that the Magic traveled everywhere on their own charter jet, so I guess I shouldn't complain. It's a real nice plane with three couches and seventeen individual reclining, swiveling seats. That's more than enough room for normal-sized people, but once a dozen NBA players get on the space tends to fill up pretty fast.

The first time I was on the plane, I claimed one of the couches, figuring that if you're 7'1", 303 pounds you automatically deserve a couch.

Someone said to me, "No way. Rookies don't get a couch."

And I said, "Bro, I'm sitting my butt down on this couch and I ain't goin' nowhere."

As I told you before, I don't like that rookie thing thrown up in my face all the time. Maybe if he would've asked me nice I would've given it up.

But I don't think so.

We usually sit in the same general places on the plane. I share the couch with Litterial, or Phi Dog as we started calling him. (Our fraternity was Phi Kappa Knuckleheads which is where the name comes from.) We usually share the couch if we're awake, but, for sleeping, the floor is real comfortable, even for someone my size. Across from us, Dennis and Nick share a couch, too. The coaches have the other couch in their section. Not much happens on these flights. I usually sleep or write rap lyrics.

In Seattle, our first stop, I had what the press called my first bad game. All right, I'll accept that. I had only 9 points and 11 rebounds, the first time I didn't get double figures in both categories. We lost 116–102. It was an example of what happens when you start to have a little success in the NBA. Teams really come to play hard against you, which is what Seattle did. That's what makes somebody like Michael Jordan such a special player. Every single night in every single city in every single season, some dude comes out to make his reputation by stopping Michael Jordan. And almost every single night, Michael puts him down.

A lot of people were comparing me to Seattle's Shawn Kemp, who had also begun his NBA career (a few years earlier) at the age of twenty. And Shawn didn't even play any college ball. I'll accept the comparison. I like Shawn, good guy, can jump out of the gym, even blocked my first shot in this game. (Though I got two of his in a row later.) But just because Shawn and I made it at that age doesn't mean everyone can. One thing I'm not going to do is hang a sign around my neck that says NBA ADVICE COUNSELOR. It's a really tricky subject about whether someone should come out of college early or not. Some guys, like Shawn, are ready for the NBA after high school. Some guys, like me, get tired of the college game after a while because it becomes impossible to grow as a player. But other guys are not ready and need the full four years. My only advice is: Look inside yourself, talk to your parents, talk to your coaches. That's the way to make a correct decision. When I was thinking about coming out after my sophomore year my father asked me why. "To make money," I said. "Not a good enough reason," he said. So I went back and came out the next year, when I had a good reason.

After the Seattle game most of the talk was about how Michael Cage had "stopped" Shaq. Well, Michael Cage is a good defensive player, but he didn't "stop" me. He got help from Shawn, he got help from Derrick McKey, he got help from a lot of people. Anyone who knows basketball knows that Michael Cage cannot stick me one-on-one. But I guess that's what's going to be written and I can't stop it.

George Karl, the Seattle coach, said something about me that stuck with me. He said I had "Larry Bird eyes," meaning scary eyes that tell everybody I've come to play. I like that. I'll remember that.

We flew to Los Angeles the next day and I went right over to tape the *Arsenio Hall Show*. Joyce, Arsenio's talent coordinator, had been after me to do the show for a long time. And finally I said, "For me to go on the show you have to let me bring my friends on and let us rap." She checked it out with Arsenio and he said, "Fine, let 'em do it."

I'll tell you how rap got started for me. A long time ago I can remember listening to my father's tapes—the Commodores, some soft jazz, a little Motown. My mom listened to the same thing. It was all right but it just didn't move me, know what I mean? I never criticized it or anything but that's the way it was. I'm sure it was the same thing for my dad and his parents.

And then I heard my first rap song, "Planet Rock." I can't remember how old I was but we were still living in New Jersey and I used to listen to 98.7 Kiss FM out of New York. They were one of the first stations to devote a lot of air time to rap. And rap just stayed with me from then on.

There's a lot of great rappers I listened to, like Heavy D and Jazzy Jeff and the Fresh Prince. But eventually I got really drawn to a group called Fu Schnickens. They're a unique bunch of guys. One raps like a character, one raps real fast, and the other is like a hard rapper. I liked them from the first moment I heard them. A couple months after I got drafted a reporter asked me who my favorite rap group was and I told him Fu Schnickens. They either read the article or heard about it and called me up. We talked for a while and eventually I brought them down here to see if we could do a song together.

Fu Schnickens means "expert of the lyrical teachings," or something like that. It sounds pretty mystical but actually they're from Brooklyn. That's okay, there can be mystical dudes from Brooklyn. They each took the name Fu. On their album cover they're dressed in martial arts suits. Chip Fu, Moe Fu, Poc Fu, and Kung Fu.

The song we did was "Can We Rock? Yeah, What's Up Doc?" It's about how I can rock as a basketball player and they can rock as MCs. A lot of people don't know how a rap song comes together. Usually what happens is that a producer writes a beat, and then you write the words to go with the beat.

94

For "What's Up Doc?" a dude from Canada named K-Cut did the beat and we did the lyrics. We worked really well together and I was proud of the job I did. I'm not saying I'm as good as the true Fus. I'm an amateur rapper. But some amateurs are pretty good at what they do, and I think that describes me. Thre's a lot of guys in the league who are really good rappers, like Cedric Ceballos of the Suns, Brian Shaw of the Heat, Tony Campbell of the Knicks, and, of course, my own partner in crime, D. Scott. We're all gonna get together for an NBA rap record one of these days.

Anyway, Fu and I put the song together and we were ready to do it on Arsenio. I was decked out with a bunch of gold chains, my rapping look, but before we went on, Leonard said, "Look, Shaq, can we compromise a little here?" Leonard's got to be concerned with my corporate image and I respect that. So I took off the chains and wore more conservative jewelry, a real nice bracelet and a ring. We did it, we were good, Arsenio liked us, the studio audience liked us. It was a success. But the reports I've heard that I want to give up basketball and concentrate on rap are just not true. I know which side my bread is buttered on, and when you're seven feet tall you can't make no living bouncing around a stage, I don't care how graceful you are.

On December 3 we lost to the Clippers 122–104. Ken Norman really went off on us with 33 points. That's how tough the NBA is. You take a player like Ken Norman, never an All-Star, the average fan doesn't even know his name, yet's he three times better than most of the guys you go up against in college. I had 26 points, but that didn't make me feel any better about the loss. That was the first time I went up against Stanley Roberts since we scrimmaged against each other at LSU. We had a couple of fights during practice because he tried to throw around elbows once in a while but nothing very serious. I don't know if he became jealous of me or not at LSU. I know when I first got to school most of the attention was focused on him and Chris Jackson, and then, when it shifted to me, Stan left and went to play in Europe. But he's basically a good guy. He had been voted the Magic's most popular player the year before, an award that I got later this season.

Our third and final game on the trip was a 119–104 loss to Golden State. I had 17 and 17, but Chris Mullin had a big game for them with 31 points and they tuned us up pretty easily. People wonder why teams don't do better on the road, but it became clear to me early in the season. I had my routine down pretty well by then—press conference, same questions, shoot-around, two cheeseburgers, fries, a couple Pepsis, sleep, go play the game, talk to the media. But that doesn't mean there aren't all kinds of distractions no one sees.

Like autographs, for example. There are people looking for autographs all over the place, after practice, around the bus, in the hotel lobby, in the coffee shop (that's why I like room service), even outside your room if they can get there. One thing I like is when a hotel assigns you a security guy and *he's* asking you for autographs. That happened a lot. I'm sure there are people who would ask you for an autograph during the game if they thought they could get your attention. Actually, something like that almost happened. In the beginning of the season I would always go out before the game to shoot around. Some players do, like Scott Skiles, others don't, but I thought it might be something I'd like to get into. But when I did it at New Jersey in the fifth game of the year, people were literally coming out of the stands to ask me to sign, and security wasn't doing anything about it. Imagine if you're a normal working guy and you're sitting at your desk and suddenly a bunch of people come in while you're on the phone and ask you to sign an autograph. So, I stopped coming out before games and I doubt if I'll ever get back to it.

The first few times you sign an autograph, naturally, it's a cool thing. I remember the first time somebody asked me for one was during a high school game in San Antonio. We were playing in a real small town in Texas and just finished beating somebody like 182–20, and a student from the other school asked me to sign. I said okay, and next thing I knew there were dozens and dozens of people around, people my own age, sticking out papers and yearbooks. It was hard for me to understand because I never thought enough of anybody to ask for his autograph, much less a high school player. But maybe they thought of me as someone older because I was so big. Or maybe they just didn't have enough to do that night.

My philosophy about autographs is this: I'll sign them if I can. But there's a lot of times I can't. One thing I usually insist on doing if there's enough time is personalizing the autograph, and so I'll ask the person his or her name. That makes some people feel real good. But it makes other people feel bad, and that's the people I'm *trying* to make feel bad. Those are the people who want your autograph just so they can sell it. See, I finally figured out that trading-card shops won't buy an autograph from someone if it says "To Billy, from Shaquille" because it's personalized and therefore worth money only to somebody named Billy. But if I sign something with just my name on it, anyone can sell it to anyone else.

The other thing that makes me mad is when you go to a city and see the same people getting stuff signed over and over. They're trying to insult my intelligence like I don't know they're there to make money off my name. I'll say, "I just signed for you, Homes. Remember?" And he'll get mad at me. It's like what happened with Charles Barkley this season. A woman asked him for an autograph and he gave it to her. But, no, that wasn't enough. She wanted two autographs. So, obviously, she wasn't a person who really wanted an autograph, a true fan of Charles's, but, rather, a person who wanted to take advantage of a public figure. So Charles poured beer on her and that made him, in some people's opinion, a bad guy.

I wish I didn't have to have this attitude about autographs. I wish autographs were for little kids to take home, sleep with at night, or put up on their wall in a nice frame. But they're not. Many of them are for adults, for profit. And that's a shame. Maybe, to make these people feel bad, I should write what I used to write when a little kid would ask me for my autograph in college: "Listen to your mother." But I doubt that they'd even get it.

I'm not denying there's a couple of original autograph-seekers out there, though. One woman came up to me, stuck out her booty, and asked me to sign on the left side. She was wearing a pair of extremely tight jeans. Believe it or not, I didn't do it. I could see me signing and then getting arrested for sexual harassment or something. No way; not me, brother.

Now you're probably thinking: how much of a distraction are women on the road? And would I tell you the whole truth, anyway? Well, nobody tells you the whole truth, bro, even if they say they do. But I can tell you that it's not nearly as wild and crazy as some people believe. When I first got here everybody told me, "After the game there are going to be a whole bunch of girls waiting for you in every city." I really haven't seen that, honestly. There's just as much chance of some ugly fat guy being there with an autograph pad as somebody like that young woman in the tight jeans.

But, sure, there are women around and I know the dos and don'ts. Most groupies I see, with makeup caked on their faces, chasing me, just turn me off. I don't care how fine, how pretty they are, if a woman chases me with that stuff on her face, I won't mess with her. I want a natural, pretty woman, and most natural, pretty women aren't off chasing athletes around a hotel lobby. Women have ways of getting your room number, too, and they'll call once in a while. If I'm in a city I'm not familiar with, I'll usually turn my phone off right away and avoid the problem. But I have to keep it on when I get to L.A. or New Jersey or the Houston area because I'm expecting calls from friends and family. So sometimes I get hassled that way.

I have a girlfriend—she knows who she is and I don't have to tell the world—and I don't need to mess around from city to city. Sure, I like to go into clubs and look, I won't deny that. But I go mainly because I love the music. I'm not attracted to women who come up and start grabbing me and asking me for stuff. My father's words always come back to me. "Don't sign nothing without reading it. Don't say yes to nothing without thinking about it. Use common sense, and you'll be all right."

Anyway, strange stuff can happen to you anywhere, not just on the road. One day in Orlando, a lady in her mid-forties shows up at my doorstep in the morning, something obviously very wrong with her head. She was either drunk or on drugs, or, maybe more scary, she was being her regular self. Anyway, she barged in past Dennis and started hollering about how she had to see me. He tried to grab her but she got into the house and just about ran me over and jumped on my back in the hallway. I mean, can you imagine acting like that? Dennis had to grab her and throw her out the door.

That's why, when I'm home, I'm always suspicious of adults. If there's a knock on the door and it's a kid, I'll usually say "Come on in." If it's an adult, I'll usually say "Whatta you want?"

• • •

We came home from the trip but things on the court didn't improve. We lost to the Celtics 117–102. I had 26 points and 15 rebounds on Robert Parish, but he had 17 and 10 and played a pretty good game. I look at Robert Parish, who was thirty-nine years old at the time and in the league for seventeen years, and I know I'll never make it that long. They'd be calling me Pops by then and I'd be sitting around boring rookies with stories of how I dunked on Karl Malone. Don't want that.

It was around this time that we cut Chris Corchiani and settled on Litterial as our backup point guard to Scott Skiles. I felt good for Phi-Dog, who was my close friend, and bad for Chris. Basketball is a business and it was a business decision. Chris made more money than Litterial, so he's the one who had to go. And I'll tell you this: Chris Corchiani can play. He can hit a trey with the best of them and he can dish it off with the best of them. I liked playing with Chris. And he'll be back in the league, I'm sure of that.

On December 9 we took our first trip to the Palace at Auburn Hills and the Pistons beat us 108–103. We made 14 three-pointers, but Joe Dumars was just as hot for them and scored 38 points. I fouled out with 1:13 left after getting 17 and 11. The play I got whistled for was an offensive foul call, my second in a row. Sometimes I think they're just looking to call that, particularly when there's a flopper like Bill Laimbeer on the floor. I really wanted to beat them. In the third period I even dove over the press table to try to save a ball going out of bounds, and after the game Olden Polynice of the Pistons said how much that impressed him. I always play like that, O.

I was in high school when I first heard about the Bad Boys, which is what the Pistons were called in the late-Eighties. I don't know what they are now but I still consider them the Semi-Bad Boys. In those days somebody would go up for a dunk and they'd just tackle the guy. I never liked the Bad Boys, never cheered when they won their two championships in 1989 and 1990. It's not my style. To me, there's a difference between a hard foul and just trying to hurt somebody, and a lot of the Pistons, like Laimbeer, didn't know the difference and still don't. In this game in December I went up in the air one time and Laimbeer just hit me in the face. No call. It's Detroit's philosophy that if you foul on every play, the refs are going to get tired of blowing their whistle and you'll get away with a lot.

The league has to do something about cheap-shot artists because they're going to hurt somebody. If I would've gotten hurt on the play where Laimbeer slapped me, I'd be out for however many games and Laimbeer would only be fined. Fines are nothing. Suspensions hurt. How about suspending a player for as long as the guy he hurt has to be out? Like later in the season when John Starks of the Knicks laid out Kenny Anderson. He got fined $10,000, while Kenny Anderson missed half the season and the Nets really needed him.

I know my feelings about the Pistons started with that first game and carried over to March 30 when I was thrown out for fighting Laimbeer and Alvin Robertson in Orlando. I might've been wrong, I might've been right, but I don't think they'll mess with me from now on. (Just kidding.)

Two nights later we got our first look at the Phoenix Suns with Charles Barkley. They were really hot at the time and stayed hot, finishing the season with the league's best record. We lost 108–107 and I felt bad because I missed two free throws down the stretch. I was at the line, needing to make both for a tie. I hit the first, then stroked the second just perfectly. But it missed. I had 26 points and 17 rebounds but it didn't matter. I missed the chance to win the game and that's what I was thinking about. Charles had kind of a quiet game with 18 points and he really didn't say much on the court, either. Somebody asked me if I was going to make Charles an honorary Knucklehead. Nah, I said, he's too old.

Well, at this point, we were ten days into December and we hadn't won a game all month. Six straight losses. That was tough to handle. Six losses was just about a season's worth at LSU and, in high school, I had lost exactly one game in two years. You have to adjust to losing right away or it'll drive you crazy. In this league you play so many games that you really don't have time to dwell on a single loss or a couple of losses. I knew we'd turn it around eventually. And we did, finally, when we beat Philly at home, 119–107. It was a real good game for us because the scoring was balanced. Dennis had 25 points, Nick had 21, I had 20, and Jeff Turner had 22. Jeff has one of the best outside shots in the league, particularly for a guy who's 6′9″, kind of an old-fashioned set shot that makes him, when he's hot, as hot as anybody in the league.

We made Jeff a Knucklehead even though he's not real young (thirty years old), not real crazy, not real nutty, and he pretty much follows directions. All in all, a real cool guy, a down-to-earth guy, a great guy but not a Knucklehead type. But we told Jeff we were scared of having problems with the NAAWP, the National Association for the Advancement of White People, and we had to let a white boy in.

While I'm on the subject of Knuckleheads, this was the first game that Tom Tolbert started at power forward for us. He had 9 points, 6 rebounds, and zero assists, one less than me. I like having Tom in there because his passing makes me look like Magic Johnson. Just kidding, Tom. A lot of people think Tom would be a Knucklehead because he has the reputation for being one of the craziest guys in the league. He once fed his young brother dog food, for example, just to see what would happen. But Tom is not a Knucklehead. He's a Surfer and that's a different category altogether. Surfers wear "No Fear" gear, they wear funny hats, they tell corny jokes, and they play euchre, a horrible, horrible card game, with Scott Skiles.

When you play against the Sixers that means you're going to see Manute Bol, which is always interesting. Think of shooting over a telephone pole and that's what it's like to play against a guy who's 7'7". He only played twelve minutes but you tend to think he's out there the whole game. When you play against Manute, you've got to take it right to him. I tried a turnaround jumper once and he blocked it. But if you go strong, you can get by him because telephone poles don't move very much. Manute's always talking out there, too, but it doesn't matter much because you can't understand what he's saying. Must be one of those African dialects or something.

The Philly game got us back in a groove and we won three more in a row after that. First, we beat the Sacramento Kings at home 112–91. I had 22 points, 20 rebounds, and 7 blocked shots, pretty close to a triple-double. I guess if I really concentrated on it, I could get double figures in blocks. But then I really wouldn't be doing my job on defense, which most of the time means protecting my turf under the basket, helping everyone else out, changing shots, and staying alert for everything, not just the guy shooting the ball.

Then we really beat up on the Hawks, in Atlanta, 125–84. Dominique Wilkins was hurt at the time and he didn't play, which had something to do with it. We went a day early and Dennis Scott and I went to a big party where we met Bobby

Brown (without his wife, Whitney Houston) and TLC, a really good girl singing group. Dennis knew a lot of people from Georgia Tech and I have a lot of friends in the Atlanta area, too. In fact, I went to the Hawks before the game and asked them for a few extra tickets. "Fine," they said. "Here's what it'll cost." Most teams will just give you the tickets, particularly since—I'm being honest and realistic here, not just cocky—I'm helping them fill their own house. Atlanta is not a great pro basketball city in terms of supporting the Hawks. I never had any real trouble dealing with any teams all year, but the Hawks got me angry and I almost got arrogant on them. Personally, I was glad when we stomped 'em.

We came back home and beat the Utah Jazz 101–98 on December 22, a nice Christmas gift for ourselves. I was happy with my game—28 points, 19 rebounds, 5 blocks. We made our big fourth quarter run with a lineup of Litterial, Steve Kerr (who came over to us from Cleveland when we released Corchiani), Donald Royal, and Jeff Turner on the floor with me. It was fun. Karl Malone had 30 points and 12 rebounds but we had him under control a lot of the game.

I don't know what it was with Malone, but every time I heard him talk about me he didn't have a single nice thing to say. "Shaq's just another player." "Ain't nothing special about Shaq." I don't really care what he thinks about me, but he seemed to be going out of his way to say it.

Funny, but when I was just starting to watch the NBA, The Mailman was one of the guys I thought was just unstoppable. And then when I got here on the same court with him he disappointed me a lot. He's a pretty good player, I guess, but kind of a baby. The main thing he does is flop and complain to the referees, and it's a good thing he's got John Stockton to get him the ball. There are other players in the league like that, but I'm not going to say who they are. At least, they're good guys and I like them. But not Karl.

I decided I wanted to do something for Christmas along the lines of Shaqsgiving. First, we donated a bunch of toys and cards to the Salvation Army. Then we got a list of needy families with about two hundred kids altogether. The list had the parents' names and the names and ages of the kids. So my elves, people like Dennis Tracey and a couple homeboys from San Antonio, went over to Toys "R" Us and bought like $4,000 worth of gifts: Sega Genesis games, skateboards, remote-control cars, racetracks, radios, cameras, all good stuff. Fortunately, Dennis and I are toy experts. After Kenner sent over that bunch of toys, anyone who came into our house the next week was likely to get shot in the head by a Nerf arrow or a water pistol or something. So we knew what to buy. Then we brought it all back to the house and wrapped it ourselves. We knew that was the only way a fifteen-year-old boy wouldn't land up with a Barbie doll or something.

On December 21 we took it over to the home for the underprivileged families and handed it out. I wore a Santa cap and everybody called me Shaq-a-Claus. It was fun.

Just like on Thanksgiving, the event got some publicity, and I heard some people whispering that I was only doing charity things to get ink in the newspapers. How do you argue with something like that? Why should I have to justify myself? But I guess I will anyway. See, there's a lot of athletes, dozens of them, who get involved in charities they don't know anything about. Their name goes on the charity's letterhead, and they show up at a dinner (maybe), and they get all kinds of credit for being "actively involved" in fighting something they don't even understand. I don't want to do that. People call Dennis Tracey all the time and ask if I can get involved in this and that, and I'll be honest with them. "Look, I'm sure it's a great cause you're fighting for but I don't know anything about it," I'll tell them. "Let somebody who knows something about it go to bat for it."

What I get involved in is what I can see with my own eyes. Homelessness. Hungry kids. Kids without loving parents. You can think what you want about what I'm involved with, but always remember that I'll be *involved*. I'll be down there carving the turkey or handing out the presents. That's the only way I could do something without feeling guilty about it.

We didn't have another game until December 26 and my first thought was just to take it easy and hang out alone in Orlando for Christmas. I got home from practice on the twenty-third at about one o'clock in the afternoon and I was just sitting there by myself. Dennis had gone home to Louisiana, everybody had gone home. So I stood up and said, "I'm going home, too." My parents had already invited me, of course, but I thought it would be too tiring since we had a game in Miami the day after Christmas. But, finally, I just threw a few things in a bag and took off. I don't think I would've been lonely in Orlando. I would've listened to music, put on a video, made an elaborate meal from one of my two hundred cookbooks. Yeah, right. Maybe that's what made me go—the thought of eating Christmas dinner at Denny's when I knew my mom would be cooking up a storm.

So I hopped on a plane and showed up in San Antonio. My mom cried. My dad just smiled. He said he had a feeling I was going to make it home.

Christmas was always a nice holiday when I was growing up, but I can't say I stayed up all night on Christmas Eve wondering what I was going to get. That's because I knew I wasn't getting much. There just wasn't enough money and my father was smart enough not to blow the family budget buying us gifts. But this year I made sure everybody got what they wanted because I handed out checks. I didn't have time to buy presents, but it's pretty hard getting stuff for your family anyway. My mom bought me a few things, like cologne and shirts, but I'm kind of like my father in that respect. I don't want anything. As long as people around me are happy, I'm happy. I'm too big for presents anyway. And when my mom brought out the turkey, macaroni and cheese, and pies, that was enough presents for me.

For the three nights I was at home, I stayed in my old bedroom, back with my brother Jamal, and I can tell you things were a little tight. I was glad I did the family Christmas but that didn't make it easy when I had to get up at five A.M. on the twenty-sixth for a six A.M. flight to Miami. In fact, I beat the team to the arena for shootaround, so I went to sleep on the floor. That's where they found me, racked out on the arena floor. I admit it—I was tired for that game, felt like I was running in quicksand. I only had 18 points and 11 rebounds and we lost 106–100. Everything in the NBA has a price. Even Christmas dinner.

We split the final two games of 1992 at home, beating the Bucks 110–94 and losing to the Lakers 96–93. On New Year's Eve, a bunch of us got all dressed up in new suits, rented limos, and went over to Jerry Reynolds's club in Eatonville, a suburb of Orlando. We just sat around talking, listening to the music and hanging out till four A.M. I don't need to drink beer or wine or get liquored up to have a good time. There are two positions I've always played pretty well—center and designated driver.

CHAPTER EIGHT

Making Noise in Charles's House

On January 2, I officially made Dennis Rodman of the Pistons a Knucklehead.

We played them at home and Dennis showed up with the words "Pro Choice" shaved into his head. Once, when he was at the foul line, he turned to the crowd and clapped his hands when they booed him. A couple other times he just laid down on the floor after not getting calls he thought he should've had. Sometimes when his coach, Ronnie Rothstein, was talking to the team during time-out huddles, Rodman deliberately faced the opposite direction to show he isn't listening to him.

All in all, an outstanding Knucklehead performance.

Some people wonder why I can like a person like Dennis Rodman because, unless things got a lot crazier than I could ever imagine, I wouldn't do the things he does out on the court. See, I'm kind of a combination Knucklehead/nice person/good citizen. I like to act crazy and follow my own instincts and do what I want. But I also don't like to show people up. I would never act up against my coach in public because that would be showing him up. And if I did some of the things Dennis did, I'm sure I'd hear my father's voice in my ear: "Boy! You lift your sorry ass off that floor and start playing. Now!"

But I don't think Dennis Rodman is nearly as crazy as some people say. I've talked to him, and he's having a lot of problems.

I'll tell you what I noticed, though: Dennis didn't show up for shootaround that morning and Ronnie Rothstein still played him. They know how much he means to that team.

Anyway, the Pistons beat us 98–97 in a real tough game. I told you before I don't like some members of that team, but they've got a couple real good players. Joe Dumars is one of them. This time he lit us up for 32. They used to have a guy named Vinnie Johnson who was called "Microwave" because he heated up fast. I call Dumars "Desert."

The Knicks came to town on January 8 for a TNT game and it was really a big one for us. We had that one-point loss to the Pistons and a three-point loss to the Nets a few nights later and we really needed a win. There was a lot going on at this time. I was leading Patrick Ewing in the fans' balloting for All-Star center and it was a big story in New York because Patrick had been the starting center in the East for the last three seasons. There was even talk that the Knicks were going to hold kind of a "registration voting party" so more New York fans would support Patrick. I didn't get caught up in it but, before the game, Patrick said to one of our clubhouse attendants: "Can you believe Shaq is beating me?" Well, yeah, I could.

I told you I don't like to get caught up in the one-on-one matchup thing very much, but it was important for me to play better against Patrick than I did in Madison Square Garden in

November. I knew I was a better player in January than I had been in November. And I know Patrick wanted to come to town and show up this rookie who was stealing some of his thunder.

Well, we beat them 95–94 in one of our best games of the season. That's because we got behind early, 22–10 and still trailed 79–67 in the fourth period but didn't give up and came right back at them. A lot of teams hate to play the Knicks, but I love it. There's lots of shoving, lots of banging, lots of talking. My kind of game.

Dennis Scott hit a big three-pointer at crunch time and I was really hot in the fourth period when I scored 11 of my 22 points and blocked three of Patrick's shots. Patrick had a short jumper at the buzzer to beat us but I was in his face and he missed. Afterward, he was pretty hot about it. "I got fouled before I got the ball and I got fouled when I took the shot," he said. That's not the way I saw it, of course. He had his arm wrapped around me and I was just trying to get around him to defend it. Anyway, what Patrick should remember is that I had five fouls a lot of the game and had to sit out much of the third period. It was typical—the loser was mad, the winner was glad. We finished pretty even statistically just like we did that first time in New York. He had 21 points, 12 rebounds, 1 blocked shot; I had 22, 13, and 5.

Maybe playing the Knicks does wear a team out more than I realized because we looked worn out against the Pacers the next night and lost 104–88. I came close to a triple-double again (30, 20, and 8) but it didn't do us much good. And three nights after that was that first game against Michael and the Bulls that I started to tell you about in Chapter 1.

After Michael blocked that first shot on me, maybe everybody thought it was going to happen every time, because I only got nine more shots the entire game. I made eight of them but finished with only 19 points, which wasn't nearly enough as we lost 122–106. It was one of those games where I thought I could do a lot more but didn't get the chance. Part of the problem, I'll admit, was that Scottie Pippen came to double me every time, holding up those long, elastic arms that make him look like a prehistoric bird. And another part of the problem was Jordan, who was just waiting for me to get the ball so he could come and double me. A couple times I got the ball in the air and before I came down—whoosh!—it was gone, almost like that Vegas magician, David Copperfield, touched it with his cane. I turned around to see who it was and it was Jordan. You can watch a guy on TV and think he's quick, but Michael is much, much quicker in person. Michael only had 23 points, the number on his jersey, but they got a real good game from Horace Grant, who had 26 points. That's the way it is with championship teams—somebody falls down, somebody steps back up. I blocked one of Michael's shots but he made a noise like "Agg-hhh!" and they called it goaltending. When Michael Jordan goes "Agg-hhh!" the rest of the NBA says, "Mike, what's the matter?"

We went up to Boston for a game against the Celtics on January 15 and, naturally, everybody wanted to know what I thought about Boston Garden, like it was the Leaning Tower of Pisa or something. What I thought was, it's a building. But I do realize the tradition because it's one of the places my father always talked about. Playing there probably meant more to him than it did to me. I could see the banners. I could sense the tradition. I could still smell Red Auerbach's cigar smoke from thirty years ago.

The first thing I wanted to know when I got there was whether or not Larry Bird was around. Unfortunately, it turned out he was down in Florida at his vacation home. I guess even he doesn't like Boston weather in the winter. Bird had retired right before the season, and I'm sorry I never got the chance to play against him.

It's funny, but when I was young I never used to like Bird. And it had nothing to do with the white-black thing because I'm not into that. I just thought that he was lucky. I saw him one time get the ball, fall on his back, shoot it over the backboard, and it went in. I felt some players were just lucky and he was one of them.

Also, when I was in Germany, I had a white kid I used to play one on one with a lot named Mitch Ryals, who thought he was Larry Bird. He was about 6'6" then and I was about 6'8" and he used to beat me all the time. I'd always pretend I was Dr. J., but Mitch was a lot closer to being Bird than I was to being Doc. Mitch was skinny like Bird, real slow, and he'd do the same things Bird did. Fake right and go left, up-and-under moves, take real crazy shots that went in, make people look silly and get them frustrated. I just couldn't stop his shot and I could never figure out why. I'm sure guys in the NBA used to say the same thing about Bird. "Man, I'm right in this slow dude's face and he's just killin' me." It was only later on when I realized that he was a hard worker, very fundamentally sound, and with a lot of skills. I've still never met him, but he said some nice things about me, and I appreciated it.

The Celtics are a great organization with lots of tradition, but I don't know whether I'd like to play forty-one games a season in Boston Garden. It was kind of cold out there in the beginning because of the ice that's right underneath the basketball court. I guess you get used to it, though. Robert Parish and I had a great battle. I had a couple monster dunks on him and he put in a couple of his tricky hooks and that rickety, high-arching fallaway jumper. In the third quarter I blocked one of his shots and his momentum carried him into the stands. He came back with catsup on his shorts.

I had one interesting call made on me. I blocked a shot by Kevin Gamble and a referee out by the midcourt line called a foul, even though the ref right next to the play saw it was clean. When I asked the ref about it, he said, "I thought you got him with your body." And I said, "Oh, we're making thought calls now?"

I didn't say it too loud, though.

We won by a pretty comfortable margin, 113–94. I had a pretty solid game with 22 points, 12 rebounds, and 4 blocked shots, but Parish had some nice numbers, too, with 19, 11, and 2. Scott Skiles had a good game for us, but the big story was Anthony Bowie, who played because Dennis was hurt, and scored 23 points. I was happy for A.B., who's a great guy, a great player to have on the team whether he's on the court or not. During the season we had this joke where we'd rub baby oil on ourselves and pose in front of the mirror like those body builder dudes. A.B. looks the best because he's got about 1 percent body fat. Anthony's a family man, and sometimes I even envy him a bit. I love his son, little A.B., I love his small daughter, Brook Ashley, and his wife, Michelle, is a nice lady. If I ever get married, I'd probably want to marry someone like her. She reminds me of my mother a little bit—real quiet, real sweet.

The way we knew we were really in control of the game was when Greg Kite shot a technical foul for us late in the game. It was a great gesture because Greg used to be a Celtic and everyone is always on his case about his bad free-throw shooting. I know how that feels. Compared to Greg, I sometimes look like Mark Price or Ricky Pierce at the line. But Greg made this one and the crowd loved it. Greg's another family man, lives a life completely different from my own, and we would never hang out. I see him at practice and games and that's it. But, in a way, that's what sports is all about. A lot of different types of people, people who don't necessarily have anything in common, coming together for one cause.

One other thing about Greg: He is probably the only person to have played against both Wilt and me. When he was a freshman recruit at UCLA about fifteen years ago Wilt still came over for pickup games even though he was in his forties. Greg said he didn't play much but he saw enough to tell me, "Shaq, you woulda chewed up Wilt and spit him out for lunch." Okay, he really didn't say that at all, but it sounded good, right, Greg?

On January 16 we went into Chicago and beat the Bulls 128–124 in one of the strangest games of the year. First of all, just beating the two-time defending champions at home is strange. But this is the game that Jordan went off with 64 points, the most I had ever seen anyone score, and we still beat them. You have a choice when you play Chicago and neither of the options is very good. You can double-team Jordan, try to hold him below, say, thirty points, and take the chance that he won't get the ball to Scottie, Horace, or B. J. Armstrong and have them all go off on you. Or you can just let Jordan get his point by single-covering him and try to stop everybody else. First, we tried to double him, but he was too quick for us and got his shots off anyway. So then we decided to let him go and play solid defense on everyone else.

Believe it or not, he hurt his wrist in this game but came back with a wristband and just kept shooting. He wasn't talking at all, just shooting and shooting. I only got one of his shots all night and they called it goaltending. I knocked him down once, too, which the fans really don't like very much in Chicago. It's kind of like if you went up to Mickey Mouse and knocked him on his butt right in the middle of the Magic Kingdom.

Michael finally stopped shooting at forty-nine, which is a lot of shots, but Nick hit a big three-pointer to send it into overtime, and we outplayed them in the five-minute extra period. After the game Michael said: ''We could learn something from the Magic. They kept battling and battling, and we were really complacent.'' Thanks, Mike. Of course, by the end of the year, you and the Phoenix Suns were the only teams battling and battling, and the Orlando Magic was watching you on TV.

I was real happy with my game there. I had 29 points and 24 rebounds, which is a big improvement over the game when they beat us in Orlando. Bill Cartwright, their center, said after the game that the Bulls had done everything in their power to shake me. The fans went at me big-time, the players doubled me hard, some of them talked a little trash, and I ignored it all. I love to hear that because, most of the time, that's what I try to accomplish out there. I love to ignore all the extra stuff, just focus in on what I have to do, and shut everybody up with my play.

After the game, Nick, who's from Chicago, took us to his club, which is called The Clique. We went upstairs to the VIP Room and just chilled. Michael and his good friend from the Bears, Richard Dent, came in, said hi and left. It was nice to come out on top of Michael in Michael's town, because it doesn't happen that much.

•   •   •

It was around this time, thirty games into the season, that I started hearing about "the rookie wall." I heard so much about it I thought I was going to wake up one morning staring at some giant wall in my bedroom. People came up with the "wall" idea because the performance of a lot of rookies started going down around this time because we're supposed to be tired. You only play about thirty games a year in college, which barely gets you one-third of the way through an NBA season.

I think "the wall" is a lot of b.s. I think somebody came in, got tired and said, "Hey, I hit the rookie wall." And everybody started believing it, like the wall was something you can reach out and touch. It's a mental thing, not a physical thing. If you keep telling somebody, "Hey, I'm going to get tired about the thirtieth game," then you're going to get tired about the thirtieth game. But I'm a mentally strong person. I don't believe you get a case of fatigue you can't come back from. If I get tired during a game, I just do what I have to do, which is get some good rest, maybe get a vitamin B-12 shot, eat a salad, and come back strong. Last season Dikembe Mutombo supposedly hit the wall and it kept him from getting rookie of the year. Look, Mutombo got tired because he's old for a rookie, twenty-five, and he's out there in Denver where the altitude is all messed up. That mile-high air is worse for you than the heat in Orlando, which doesn't bother me at all.

Two days after beating the Bulls in Chicago, we lost to the

Angelic smile. Big, soulful eyes. The heart of a little devil.

Even as a young man I was tall, dark, and handsome. *Robert G. Cole Jr.-Sr. High School Yearbook, 1989*

It was a Magic moment for the Harrison family on the day I signed my rookie contract. From left, father Philip, sister Ayesha, mother Lucille, me, brother Jamal, sister Lateefah. *Fernando Medina*

Commissioner David Stern announces me as the first pick of the 1992 draft. Later, of course, I had to switch numbers. I'm a 32 man now. *AP/Wide World Photos*

My main man, Dennis Scott, signs autographs with me on Broadway. *Bill Frakes/ Sports Illustrated © Time Inc.*

The world's biggest rapper shows his lyrical skills on Arsenio. *AP/Wide World Photos*

Shaq-a-Claus provided holiday gifts for underprivileged kids in Orlando. *Barry Gossage*

My first NBA All-Star team, and it won't be my last. I made sure to sit next to coach Pat Riley. *1992, Nathaniel Butler, NBA Photos*

As you can see, Patrick Ewing, Wilt Chamberlain, and yours truly were overcome with joy before the ceremonial tipoff at Madison Square Garden in November. *Nathaniel Butler/Sports Illustrated © Time Inc.*

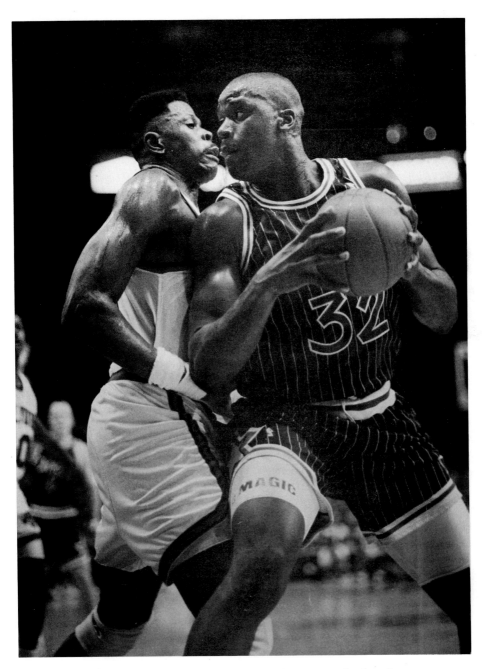

My battles with Patrick Ewing were competitive every single minute.
AP/Wide World Photos

I believe they call that a dunk. I get a few from time to time. On this play, Scott Skiles and Tom Tolbert help me out by standing around with their eyes closed. *1993, Nathaniel Butler, NBA Photos*

I'm about to show Seattle's Michael Cage my fadeaway baseline jumper. *1993, Nathaniel Butler, NBA Photos*

Hi, Christian Laettner, how ya' doing. Fine. Good. Take it out then. *Barry Gossage*

My jump hook, this one against Kevin Duckworth, is a good weapon when I'm close to the basket. *1993, Andrew Bernstein, NBA Photos*

Legs spread, knees up, Ninja yell, and it's another Shaq Attack on the basket. *Barry Gossage*

The Lakers' Anthony Peeler wants no part of this slam at the Forum. I don't blame him. He's only a guard. *1993, Andrew Bernstein, NBA Photos*

I like to smile on the court once in a while, but sometimes basketball is nothing but sweat and hard work. *1993, Nathaniel Butler, NBA Photos*

My former teammate at LSU, Stanley Roberts, looks like he's using the old elbow technique as I slip by him and get ready to dunk on Danny Manning in a game against the Clippers. *AP/Wide World Photos*

So who would be your first choice at center? From left, Bill Walton, Bill Russell, Shaq, Wilt Chamberlain, Kareem Abdul-Jabbar. The man in the front is the all-time ultimate coach, John Wooden. This photo was taken at the Reebok Legends commercial shoot. *George B. Fry III*

I guess neither Larry Johnson (2) nor Alonzo Mourning wanted to step in and take the charge. *1993, Lou Capozzola, NBA Photos*

Dennis Scott and I check out the scouting report before a game at Charlotte.
Bill Frakes/Sports Illustrated © Time Inc.

Sixers 124–118 in overtime in Philadelphia on Martin Luther King Day. Maybe we hit the wall. (Just kidding.) I always seem to have big games against the Sixers because they don't double me, and this time I had 38 points, 16 rebounds, and 8 blocked shots. But it was a weird game. We missed all eleven of our three-pointers. Jeff Hornacek was hitting all kinds of crazy shots, shots like he was in a H-O-R-S-E game or something, and finished with 32 points. 'Spoon, Clarence Weatherspoon, Philly's real good rookie forward, had a good game with 24 points, too. I don't envy 'Spoon's situation. He came in there to replace Charles Barkley and that's impossible.

We lost to the Heat a few nights later, 110–104, but fortunately the Dallas Mavericks came to town on January 23. At this time, the Mavericks were going after the worst record in NBA history and seeing them was like seeing a gallon of cold water after you been crossing the desert. We won 127–106. I had another 38-point game and made 10 of my 14 free throws, a percentage I would've gladly taken for the year. The other good news was that I didn't commit a single personal foul for the first time all season.

The victim for most of this was Sean Rooks, and I can't say I felt sorry for him. Back in college, when I played against him at Arizona, all he did was talk, talk, talk. They quadruple-teamed me the whole game and all I heard was Rooks talking and talking. And I turned to him and said, "Rooks, you can talk all you want, buddy-boy, because no matter what you say I'm gonna be a better NBA player than you." And after the game he went and told the papers, like a little girl, like someone going to their mom and saying, "Mom, here's what Shaq said. Can't you go beat him up?"

We then lost two of our remaining three games in January, leaving us with an 18–19 record and a tough five-game Western road trip coming up. I noticed that this was when everybody started writing us off, figuring that the quick start was all a fluke and that we'd be back in Lottery Land when we came home. The Magic had always had trouble on the Coast and had lost 30 of 36 games out there before I came. And then there was the 0–3 performance in December.

What did it all mean? Nothing, bro. Nothing at all.

We got a sendoff for our trip on January 30 at the annual Orlando Magic Youth Foundation black-tie dinner. Some corporate people paid out over $5,000 to have dinner with me. Heck, I would've met them over at the pizza place for nothing. But it's a good cause. I was sitting with a bunch of real nice people and they were describing how most of these society dinners go, with a lot of rich people sitting around, holding a drink with their little finger out, and saying, "Extraordinary. How extraordinary."

• • •

This trip West had a real crazy feel about it. Maybe it was because it looked like I was going to beat out Patrick for the All-Star team and that drew a lot of attention. Maybe it was because ESPN was following me around for a one-hour show they wanted to do. Maybe it's because the people out there didn't have enough to do. I don't know.

It started in Sacramento on January 31, Super Bowl Sunday, when ESPN asked me to go to a sports bar called Bleachers and watch the debut of my Reebok commercial at halftime. We were in a back room but there were so many people pushing to get in and see us that it was like a mini-riot. There were even a couple scuffles between fans and security people. So I was a little distracted when I watched the commercials, which didn't change my opinion of them. Which was:

They were good! Real good! I know, I know. Everybody in America has seen them a thousand times by now, heard me say, "Don't fake the funk . . ." watched my expression change when they handed me the dustpan. But admit it: the first time you saw the commercial, you thought it was pretty good, too, right?

The next day at shootaround I bet a guy from ESPN that I

could get through the crowds waiting at the hotel without being spotted. So when the bus stopped, I got out a jheri-curl wig I had bought back at some novelty store in Orlando. I don't know who everybody thought I was besides maybe the world's biggest reggae singer. The gig didn't last too long, though, probably because I had a Shaq Reebok jacket on, and everybody recognized me in the lobby. Every little step closer to those room service burgers helps, bro.

We started off the trip with a 119–115 win over the Kings that night in a real strange game. I was on the bench a lot of the time in foul trouble yet all the rest of the guys did was shoot fouls, 57 of them, in fact. We made 41 and that was the difference.

We went to L.A. to play the Lakers the next day and I had a real big game, making 13 of 17 shots for 31 points and getting 14 rebounds in a 110–97 win, one of the best of the season. Everybody assumed it was because I was psyched up to play in the Forum, but that wasn't the case. I was psyched up mostly because I had played a bad game in Sacramento and, as I told you before, I hate playing two bad games in a row. I simply won't let myself do it. I even had a real sore knee at the time but I wasn't going to let it stop me.

I'll admit it, though, playing at the Forum was fun. If you can't get up for games like that, you've got no business in the league. My thoughts of playing for the Lakers were all finished by then. I was a Magic man and all I wanted to do was *beat* the Lakers. Jack Nicholson was there looking at me with this mean-looking face, and when I went past him once I turned and said, "Oh, Jack, Vlade Divac can't stick me, Jack." Downtown Julie Brown was there, too. She said I was young and innocent. I said, "You're absolutely correct."

After the game a lot of celebrities were around: Ronnie Lott, Leslie Nielsen, Rob Lowe, Pete Sampras, the tennis player, Malcolm Jamaal Warner from *Cosby*, and Holly Robinson from *Hangin' with Mister Cooper*. Holly and I became friends and I saw her a few times after that. Whenever anyone would question me about it, I'd say, "Hey, I was just hangin' with Mister Cooper, bro."

L.A. was supposed to be a really cool place about dealing with athletes because there's always so many movie stars around, but I'm here to tell you that no place in the league was crazier to get out of. Somehow, a mob of people had gotten into the arena through the tunnel where the players go out and they practically tore me apart, like I was a rock star or something. Imagine if they had seen someone *real* famous, like Dennis Scott.

When I finally got out of there, I spent the rest of the night hangin' with Mister Cooper.

Another funny thing happened when I was in L.A. Leonard got a call from William Friedkin, a big-name director who made movies like *To Live and Die in L.A.* and *The Exorcist*. He wanted to know if I'd be interested in appearing in a basketball movie he was making called *Blue Chips*. I assumed I wouldn't have to play a part where my head spun around.

Bill had seen my commercials and said I had "enormous likability." I wish NBA referees felt that way. Anyway, Leonard said we'd certainly be interested in looking into it. My reaction, as usual, was kind of a nonreaction. "Sounds good, let me think about it," I said. I've learned that you can't get overly excited about some things. Some things sound good at first but, when you look into them, they turn out not to be so hot.

Fortunately, this turned out to be one of the good ones.

The next day Dennis Scott and I flew a helicopter. All right, we just rode in one. Robert Earl, a cool guy who owned the Hard Rock Cafés and is now involved in Planet Hollywood, invited us to visit this unbelievable mall in Orange County, and he figured the best way to get there was to take his chopper. We landed right on the roof of the mall, shopped for a while, bought a pair of snakeskin boots, and came back. That's style. I also bought one of these little drum sets and played it so much that everybody was ready to kill me by the end of the trip.

On February 5 we played at Portland and continued our roll with a 114–106 victory. This was right after a few Portland players had gotten involved with underage girls in a mall in Salt Lake City. There were eventually some suspensions and fines, and you could see that their team chemistry was all messed up. They were fumbling, slipping, dropping the ball, shooting airballs, missing wide-open dunks. They looked like they were playing on roller skates. So, we were 3–0 on the trip and feeling real good as we headed for Phoenix and an NBC game on February 7.

The game was a big one for our franchise because it was the first time the Magic would be appearing on network TV. In fact, NBC had originally scheduled a Celtics-Warriors game for the date but dropped them for us. Now, if Larry Bird were still playing would they have done the same thing? At the time, the Suns had an incredible 33–9 record, best in the league, but we honestly thought we could beat them. That's how well we were playing. In most of the promos, naturally, NBC billed it as ''Charles versus Shaq.'' Right. Now I'm being matched up against forwards. One of the Phoenix newspapers even had a Shaq ''tale of the tape'' with all my measurements and stuff, like it was a heavyweight boxing match.

Anyway, what you all want to know is: How did they rig the basket so it came down when I dunked 2:27 into the game, right? Okay, here's how the scam went down. The night before the game, Dick Ebersol, the president of NBC Sports called me and said: ''Shaq, we want to risk all our credibility and reputation by having you pull down the basket, and we want you to risk all your endorsement contract money and popularity by scamming the public, and we know you'll agree.''

Please. I don't want to hear about a rigged rim. I've been tearing stuff down my whole life, and now, suddenly, because the game is on NBC, they whole thing was a fake? A lot of people actually thought that and some still do. But what happened was very simple. A.B. was supposed to throw me a lob, but he shot it. The ball came off my way and I just took it and slammed it down, real hard, with my weight on the rim. Yes, I hung on the rim because someone was under me, and, as I did, the whole apparatus just started to come down slowly. Leonard was watching and he later told me it looked like something out of a science fiction movie. When I hit the floor, I just trotted away because it looked like the basket was going to land on my head. I'm glad I hadn't lifted my legs up like I do sometimes when I dunk or that stuff would've come down on my head and I would've been dead.

The game was delayed for thirty-seven minutes and Dennis and I spent some time working on our dance steps. The Suns have a spare gym near the visiting locker room and we tried to get it but they were already in it. We could hear what they were saying: "When Shaq gets the ball, you, you, and you get on him." I knew I'd have something to look forward to when I got back on the court.

Richard Dumas, a rookie whom I had never heard of, just killed us, doing chinups on the rim, hitting jump shots, tapping in balls. He had 31 points. Man, even guys you don't know can kill you in this league. For me, the game was a four-letter word. F-o-u-l. I played only twenty-nine minutes because of foul trouble, and only two minutes in the last quarter when they scored 44 points to clinch a 121–105 win. I finally fouled out with 3:16 left when they called me for fouling Kevin Johnson on a drive to the basket. I told the ref, "If I wanted to stop K.J. on a drive, I would've knocked him out of bounds." They didn't buy my logic and pointed to the sideline.

On one play, I posted up, felt the defender on my leg, spun off him real quick, and scored. Tweet! Wait a minute, no basket. Charge on the rookie. And I looked down at the defender, who happened to be Mister Barkley, and he had this real wide smile on his face.

So even Charles flops from time to time. See, I think the

league is missing a real good chance on this. Every year around Academy Award time in March or April, the league should hold its own awards show and give out prizes. We could call the awards the Laimbeers. "Ladies and gentleman, the Laimbeer for best flop in the fourth period goes to . . ." And you could give out Best Supporting Flopper, Best Foreign Flopper, a lot of different things. Make it a black-tie affair. Get a corporate sponsor, like a tuna fish company maybe.

I'll admit it. I was angry and frustrated after the game. It was the first time I told Alex Martins that I wasn't talking to the press, although I eventually came out and did it anyway. Jerry Colangelo, the Suns' president and part-owner, told me that as long as Phoenix won he wasn't going to send me a bill for the basket. After this game the NBA did start talking about a rule that would require teams to have a spare basket support ready at all times, just like Phoenix did. It would probably go down in history as "The Shaq Rule."

I wasn't happy and my teammates weren't happy, but I guess NBC was happy. Soon afterward they announced that ratings were so successful, they were adding our home game against the Spurs on February 28 to their schedule. Gee, I wondered how they wanted to rig the basket for that one . . .

We lost the final game of the trip in Utah, by 108–96, but beat the Cavs at home, 96–87. It was a very satisfying win. They have a great team and I really respect their center, Brad Daughterty. I was sick as a dog with the flu, about ten steps slow, but I got a shot of penicillin and hung in there. My rule is, if I can walk, I can play.

Alonzo Mourning and I got together at last, in Charlotte, on February 11; World War IV, I guess. The newspapers were again full of the Zo-Shaq matchup, but I liked what Zo said: "This isn't a boxing match." Everybody wanted to know how many times we met and what we had to say to each other, but, really, we didn't know each other very well at all. We had met at a couple rookie things but never really talked much. We never matched up in college and never even played against each other in high school. He went to a lot of those big-name summer camps, but Texas had a rule that players in-state couldn't attend them.

They beat us 116–107, and I thought we both did pretty well. Scott Skiles and I were killing them on the high pick-and-roll, and on one play I leaned in to dunk over Zo and Larry Johnson and strained my back a little bit. I think I could've had a big scoring night if it wasn't for that. I finished with 24 points, 18 rebounds, and 4 blocks, and Zo had 27 points, 14 rebounds, 2 blocks. He can't check me inside, no way. But he did beat me downcourt a few times and hit a few hooks over me. I give him credit. We'll both be here for a while. We're not going anywhere.

Valentine's Day was special because we were playing the Knicks at home, so I thought I'd make it special for someone else, too. There's a hospital near my house, the Arnold Palmer Hospital for Children and Women, and I sent every single woman in the hospital, all three hundred of them or something, two roses. I thought about sending a couple over to Patrick, but he might've gotten the wrong idea.

And after the game he wasn't in a rosy kind of mood—we beat them 102–100 in a triple overtime game, also on NBC.

If there was ever a game that taught me to keep on keeping on, this was it. Check out these stats. I was outscored by Patrick 30–8 in regulation. I made only 3 of 17 shots in the first four periods. I played only eight minutes in the first half because of foul trouble. They were about to send out an APB for Shaq.

But I hung around. At the end of regulation I blocked Patrick's shot to send the game into overtime. Then, in the three overtimes, I blocked six more shots and scored 13 points, and finally fouled out Patrick near the end of the first overtime. Keep on keeping on.

It's funny, but NBC never knew the Orlando Magic existed before this season. Now we've given them such great shows they might be ready to add us to their primetime schedule.

Free throws, free throws, free throws. On February 16 I got my career high, 46 points against the Pistons, but I missed 8 of 16 free throws and we lost 124–120 in overtime. Somebody told me it was the most points anyone had ever scored against the Pistons at the Palace, but what I needed more than anything was five more free throws. It hurt, I'll admit it. But when I'm asked to talk about it after the game, it's hard. What do I say? A miss is a miss is a miss. I shoot it, it doesn't go in. It's not that complicated. It's a matter of concentration. I have the mechanics, I have the ability, and I'm going to come back improved, if only so I don't have to keep talking about it.

I took twenty-five shots in the game, which is minor league for a guy like Jordan but a lot for me. I was just feeling it and a lot of the baskets were easy ones, like on fast breaks. Skiles and I had the alley-oop lob going, too. It took us a while in the beginning of the year to get it down, but, once we did, it's hard to stop if we both see it at the same time.

The lob is not really a set play, but we get it at least once a game and usually more than that. If I have a guy in the post leaning on me and bumping, the best thing for me to do is not fight him, but spin and go toward the basket, look for the lob, catch, and dunk. One day in the preseason, all of a sudden, we got it like seven times in a row. All I need is a moment to whisper in Skiles's ear: "Scott, he's leaning on me." And I know I'm going to get it. Anthony Bowie and Dennis Scott are pretty good at giving it to me on the lob, too. I tell them to throw it about a foot below the bottom of the backboard.

But the next night we came right back home and beat the Nuggets 111–99. It's always nice to rebound on back-to-backs because they can kill you. I had a pretty good game with 24 and 18, and Dikembe Mutombo had 15 and 15. I'm sorry to say this, but I think he's a dirty player. He gets the ball and goes straight for your face with that sorry-ass hook. I told him, "Mutombo, you elbow me again, I'm gonna punch you in your face.'' I couldn't block his shot, I'll say that. He got me in the neck, the face, the jaw, all over the place.

That was our last game for six days. Most of the guys were going to be getting some rest. But I had a date in Salt Lake City with some guys named Michael, Isiah, and Dominique.

CHAPTER NINE

Sittin' and Fumin' at the All-Star Game

I had been officially named to the All-Star team on February 3, the same day that Pat Riley was officially upset about it in New York City. I received a total of 826,767 votes, fourth behind Michael Jordan, Scottie Pippen, and Charles Barkley. In other words, I was the top vote-getter among guys who weren't on the Olympic team. Patrick Ewing finished second among centers in the East with 528,-368 votes. Math was not my major, but when I subtract Patrick's votes from my votes the total I get is "A lot."

But Pat Riley was mad. "It's ridiculous with what Patrick has accomplished in his career and this year that he's not the starter," Riley said. I guess I understood where he was coming from. And, if the situations would've been reversed, maybe

Matty Goukas would've said the same thing. But I don't know that for a fact. I do know that what Pat Riley said sounded like sour grapes. If I land up starting for the next six years and in the seventh some rookie comes in and beats me out, you won't hear me cry. And I doubt if you'll hear my coach cry, either. I could've understood it maybe if the voting would've been real close. But almost 300,000 votes? That meant an awful lot of people wanted to see me instead of Patrick. That doesn't make me a better player than Patrick. That doesn't mean I've proven more in my short NBA career than he has in his long one. It means that people wanted to see me in this game, and that's what All-Star teams are all about. I know I didn't have any control over it. I didn't cast a single vote. I told the papers something I've said a lot of times. "If I was a fan, I'd want to come and see Shaq play, too." I hope that doesn't sound cocky. I'm just being honest.

In fact, when people first started talking about the All-Star team early in the season, I honestly didn't know how it was picked. I didn't follow it in college and I never paid any attention to when they were talking about "the fan balloting." I thought the coaches just got together and picked it, which is the way they choose the rest of the team, the nonstarters. After I was announced, I could see I was in some select company. Only twelve other players in the history of the NBA had been picked to start in their rookie season: Bob Cousy, Tommy Heinsohn, Wilt, Oscar Robertson, Walt Bellamy, Jerry Lucas, Luke Jackson, Rick Barry, Elvin Hayes, Magic, Isiah, and Michael, who was the only rookie in the last ten years to make it. Even Larry Bird didn't get picked. I had heard of all of those guys except Luke Jackson, who I later found out was a big tough dude who played with the 76ers in the Sixties. I know Tommy Heinsohn especially. He's the Celtic broadcaster who doesn't like me and who's always on my case when we play the Celtics. "Hey, Shaq shouldn't get that call," Tommy will scream. "He's a rookie." Hey, Tom, now we're members of the same club, bro.

So when I'm real old one day I can gather all my grandkids around me and say, "Kids, there were only two rookies to start in the All-Star game in my era. Michael Jordan and your grandpa."

There's always a lot of rumors around All-Star weekend because the NBA trading deadline is a few days after the game. Before I went to Salt Lake City, there was a lot of talk about trading Dennis Scott for Jimmy Jackson. Jimmy still hadn't signed with the Mavericks by this time, remember, and they would've done almost anything to trade his rights. But I tried to make my feelings clear to the Magic. I know I'm not the general manager or the owner, but I want Dennis to stay with me. Guys like Dennis and Litterial are valuable to a team. They know their role, they only want to win, and they have personality. That's important to a team. A lot of players come to the gym, punch in, do their job, and go home. That doesn't make a winning team, like the Bulls. All those guys have personality: Jordan, Pippen, Grant. They don't always get along perfectly, but they blend together and give that team a certain style. That's what we have to get here.

Jimmy Jackson's cool and a great player and all, but that doesn't mean he's necessarily better for us. I know over in Charlotte, Larry Johnson told his bosses, "If Kenny Gattison goes, I go." That's how strong he felt about keeping Gattison with him. I'm glad it never came to that down here.

● ● ●

The Orlando Magic All-Star caravan—Pat Williams, his son Jimmy, Alex Martins, his assistant Lori Hamamoto, Dennis Tracey, Leonard, and the East's starting center—left Orlando Friday morning, February 19, for Salt Lake City. I had looked into renting a private jet for the trip but it would've cost $25,000, and I have my limits, as well as my sanity. In typical airline fashion, they never put the bag that was carrying my warmup jacket on the plane, and my warmup never made it to Salt Lake City until Sunday morning, the day of the game. Alex never told me that, which was smart of him.

The scene at the airport in Salt Lake was a little crazy. When I got in I saw David Robinson at the baggage pickup standing by himself, and I had all these people around. Everyone always wants to see the new kid on the block, I guess. That's okay, but part of me hopes that the Shaq novelty wears off. A little of it anyway.

The first official function of the weekend was a press conference in this big room where the NBA had all the players sit around at their own individual tables. There was good news and bad news for me. The bad news was that Michael Jordan decided to skip the conference, which got him a $10,000 fine. That meant some of the attention that Jordan would've gotten went to me. The good news was that sitting across the room was Charles Barkley, who had the biggest crowd of reporters. Anytime any of us started getting bored with all the questions, which for me was about five minutes after they started, the reporters knew they could dash over to Charles's table and get the real juicy stuff.

Guess what everyone wanted to ask me? Shaq, what's been the biggest adjustment? Naturally, they wanted to get into the controversy about Patrick Ewing and me. But I wouldn't bite. I just said that Patrick and I are both here, we're both going to play, and we're both going to help the East get a victory. Besides, with Pat Riley, the East coach, standing just a few feet from me at his own table, I wasn't going to start talking a lot of nonsense.

A couple of people were talking about skiing in the nearby mountains and how NBA players are forbidden to do it in the standard player contract. "Yeah," I said, "but that wouldn't stop me from going down that mountain in an inner tube." The thing is, I was serious. When I lived in Germany our house was on a real steep hill and when it snowed we'd take a hose, turn it on a little bit, let it run all night, and it would be real icy by the next day. We had these old-fashioned sleds called Flexible Flyers and we used to cut our own paths right through the trees and everything. I miss that. Maybe I'll take up bobsled-ding like Herschel Walker did. I'm sure they could use some 300-pound guy on that sled.

A lot of the reporters kept coming over to me and talking about what Isiah was saying at another table. Apparently Isiah was telling everybody that he was going to do everything possi-ble to get me the ball, see if I could dominate the game. (If only Pat Riley would've had that philosophy.) It surprised me that Isiah would do that but I appreciated it. I think he was just promoting the league, being unselfish because he knows he's near the end of his career and wants to see the NBA go on.

But there were other guys, and Karl Malone was one of them, who resented me being there. I could see it in their eyes. I'm not an idiot. I can spot a fake person all the way. Hakeem was cool. Isiah was cool. Larry Johnson was cool. Patrick was pissed. Malone was pissed.

I knew that nobody was going to freeze me out, though. If they tried, I'd just get a rebound, dribble all the way down-court, and dunk.

Later that night the NBA held a charity auction and my All-Star jersey sold for $55,000, while Michael's only went for $25,000. So I'm $30,000 ahead on charity jerseys, and three behind him on MVP awards earned and championships won.

The next day Fu and I did "What's Up Doc?" at the NBA's Stay in School Jam. Knocked 'em dead, bro, even though we didn't have time to practice. Rap's like riding a bike—once you do it, you just don't forget. I saw Paula Abdul at the Jam, said hello to her, and a little later on somebody wanted to know if we were going out. And they wonder how rumors get started. Then I went to another media session to let the other five hundred reporters who hadn't been at Friday's session ask the same questions. After practice, which was pretty basic because there's not a lot of time to put in new stuff, Isiah grabbed me for a one-on-one game. Once again, he wanted to make sure that he wasn't coming across as a veteran who was just treat-ing me like a rookie. Some of the other guys were pulling stuff like "Hey, rookie, carry the bags, please." Scottie Pippen said that. But Isiah was cool.

The weekend was great in general but, like I said, I did feel a little bit of that jealousy thing. I didn't come into the NBA to compete with Jordan or Ewing as a "personality." Some of that happened and that's the way it goes. But I came in to play basketball, make money, provide security for my family. If Chris Webber comes in here and makes more money and has more magazine covers and commercials than me, then I'm going to say, "Right on, Chris." I'm going to grab him and play one-on-one and show that there's no jealousy, just like Isiah did to me.

That evening I went to the All-Star Saturday events and watched Harold Miner win the Slam Dunk contest. He was awesome. I like Miner basketball-wise and fan-wise. Out of the first-year players, I think Miner, Mourning, Laettner, Jimmy Jackson, and myself will be the ones to take the NBA into the 21st century. In our own way, we're all different, but we all have some special quality, something about our personality, that sets us apart. Miner is like a mini-Jordan. (Maybe I shouldn't put that much pressure on him.) Mourning is a real serious player but a center with a lot of skills. Laettner is that mean white guy, like Larry Bird. Jimmy Jackson is just a great all-around player with enough different skills to really set himself apart. And me?

I'm a combination of The Terminator and Bambi, as somebody once said.

Then we all got introduced and I received my All-Star ring. It won't be the last, I know that. But this first one I wanted my father to have, so I gave it to him.

By the time Sunday night rolled around some of the fans probably forgot there was actually a game. But I can tell you the players didn't. That's why we were there. I was a little nervous, sure. I was surrounded by great players and, even though I thought I had proven myself over the first three months of the season, you have that little bit of doubt in your mind. But it pretty much goes away when the ball goes up. John Stockton said something after the game, which I think was true: "The younger guys in the game really wanted to win, and then the older guys really got competitive, too." It made for a really great game, with serious defense, and we lost 135–132 in overtime.

I got off to a quick start and felt in the rhythm of the game from the beginning. I hit three free throws, made a fifteen-foot jumper, got a dunk or two. By halftime I had 13 points in 14 minutes. But then I hardly played in the second half. I started in the third quarter, left about halfway through, and didn't get back in until just 1:54 was left in the game. Once I went back in, I stayed in for four of the five minutes of overtime, and, in fact, Patrick and I played together some of the time, me at center, him at power forward. When all was said and done, we played exactly the same number of minutes, twenty-five each.

In the locker room everybody wanted me to go off on Riley, but I wouldn't do it. "I wasn't upset," I told everybody. "I was just glad to be out there having fun." My dad was pretty angry and talked to some reporters about it, but I was not getting drawn into that trap. So I'll tell you how I feel now.

I was pissed off, no doubt about it. And the thing was, I knew exactly what Pat Riley was going to do. I knew he was going to give us equal minutes, so no one could say anything about it afterward. I even saw coach Riley and his assistants at the end of the bench going over the minutes very carefully so they'd come out about equal. I just didn't think it was fair because the fans had picked me as the starter, just like, if they picked Pat, I would expect to play fewer minutes than him. I knew Coach Riley used the fact that I was picked as motivation for his own player, maybe even thinking ahead to the playoffs when we might've met them in the first round. But at the All-Star Game, he was supposed to be coaching the Eastern Conference, not the New York Knicks.

But, once it was over, it was over. Actually, my biggest regret wasn't playing time. It was the fact that I didn't get a chance to take a three-point shot like I had promised. Maybe next year.

● ● ●

I got back to Orlando on Monday afternoon in the middle of practice, and the team gave me a real nice reception. Matty blew the whistle and everybody came over and shook my hand. It was back to work the next night, February 23, and we had a real good game beating Portland 125–107. I had 28 points, 14 rebounds, and 5 blocked shots, so I guess I wasn't tired. For some reason Cliff Robinson, Uncle Cliffie as he's known in Portland, was talking all kinds of noise, calling me "rookie" and stuff like that. I had to dunk on his head a few times to quiet him down.

The next day somebody told me about Christian Laettner getting fined $26,000 (one day's pay) for flying to North Carolina to accept an award instead of going to practice, as his team told him to. I've already told you how much I like Laettner, but I think he was wrong in this case. If the team said no, then he should've said no. When I got the James J. Corbett Award later in the year for being the best amateur athlete in Louisiana, Dennis Tracey went down to accept it for me. The Wolves are paying his salary, just like the Magic is paying mine, and that's who you owe your time to during the season.

In our final three games of February, we beat the Bullets 92–91 on Nick's three-pointer in the final second, but lost to two good teams, the Bulls, 108–106, and the Spurs, 94–90. Jordan had 36 on a bad ankle against us in the Chicago game, which meant he might've gotten 64 again on two good ankles. Jeff Turner and Scottie Pippen got into a scuffle in the last part of the game and both of them got tossed out. Jeff, next time try to get Michael pissed off at you in the first period and you'll be accomplishing something. In the Spurs game, David Robinson hit a lot of medium-range jumpers on me. I'll admit it's a problem dealing with him. I can't leave the boards that much, but somebody has to pick him up out there.

That San Antonio game was the fourth straight week I had been on NBC—tearing down the basket in Phoenix, going against Patrick in triple overtime, the All-Star Game, and a pretty good duel with David.

Maybe they should just turn me into a miniseries.

CHAPTER TEN

Turning 21

At the end of February our record was 26–25 and we were still in an excellent position to make the Eastern Conference playoffs. I was constantly being asked about the playoffs, and nobody seemed to believe me when I said I wasn't thinking about them. But I wasn't. The NBA season is so long that you've got to take it one game or, at the most, one week ahead. You didn't have to do that in college. You could point to this, this, and this game and know you were going to get a win and all you had to worry about was Duke or Georgia or Kentucky three weeks down the road. Can't do that here, bro. And I learned it early.

We started the month with a 108–89 win over the Timberwolves. Christian and I both had good games, both around 25 points, 16 rebounds. He's had a much rougher year up in Minnesota than I've had—trouble with his coaches, trouble with his teammates, trouble with reporters. I've stayed pretty much out of trouble like that and I'm not sure why. Anyway, things will straighten out for Christian. It takes some people a while to make a good impression.

Derrick Coleman was in a talking mood when we played the Nets in New Jersey on March 4. I was in foul trouble, and there was one time I didn't jump when he had an open dunk. He pointed at me and spread his hands as if to say, "Where's the lazy seven-footer?" And one other time he kind of patted me on the back after he dunked. Okay, Derrick, I thought, maybe I'll have something for you next time we play, like maybe rip a basket down on your head. They beat us 116–97, though, so I guess he could talk.

We also lost the next night at Milwaukee, 109–91, which made everyone think that a team meeting was necessary the following day. It's against my code to reveal exactly what was said, but I'll tell you my comments: "We can sit here and talk all we want, but what we really need to do is go out and do it on the court." I guess I've never been a big meeting guy because I've seen a lot of guys who talk a good game but don't really play it once the ball goes up.

But maybe it was necessary. The season is so long and sometimes so monotonous that you can just put it on automatic pilot. Sometimes it helps to sit around and hear that other guys are going through the same things you are.

Actually, March 6 was known for something else around Orlando.

Shaq turned 21.

A lot of people had wanted to do something special for me but I said no. Robert Earl wanted to close down Hard Rock and have a party for me there and someone else wanted me to celebrate at Church Street Station, which is the main shopping area of Orlando. It was nice that people were thinking about me, but I couldn't see sharing my twenty-first with thousands of people I never met.

The local paper had a number to call in and suggest what to buy me as a present. There were all kinds of crazy stuff: massages, marriage proposals, ballet lessons, a vault to put my cash. Someone wanted to cook me a meal and another joker suggested free-throw lessons. Ha, ha, ha. One man offered a Porsche from the year I was born, 1972, in exchange for an autographed ball. It sounded like a good deal until I heard that he also wanted $12,000. All together, the paper got about four hundred calls.

I didn't get any of their gifts. What I did get was real simple: a popcorn popper and a blender from my mother. She told me the blender is to make non-alcoholic drinks, which is fine with me. And I went out and bought myself a puppy, an eight-week-old Rottweiler, partly for security because Rottweilers look mean, and partly because I just wanted one. I used to have a dog when I was little but he made the mistake of biting my father one time, and the next thing I know the dog was in the doggie hospital. I named the puppy Shazam after that Saturday morning cartoon character. I just liked the name, and I'd always told myself that maybe I'd name my first son Shazam. I don't think I'll be tempted to do that now. You don't want to be having your son confused with your dog all the time. I'm a funny guy—I love puppies but I hate puppy smell. So immediately after getting Shazam I bought a case of air freshener and I'm always telling the housecleaner to use more and more of it. Dennis says our house sometimes smells like a Lysol factory.

My birthday was spent quietly, hangin' with Mister Cooper, Dennis Tracey, and another friend. We went to a movie, then went to see David Alan Grier at a comedy club. I know that for most guys who turn 21 it's a big deal to go out and buy a drink legally, but I didn't feel that way.

It's funny, though, but my first thought when I turned 21 was that I missed being 17. I remember 17 as a really great

age. I was 7'1" by then and when I went out and told people
I was just 17, they got this funny expression on their face and
said, "What?" Now, I'm still that height but I'm 21 and everybody knows who I am and it's not a surprise anymore. I used
to get carded at some clubs around Baton Rouge when I was
17 and a freshman because the drinking age was 18. Everybody knew I wasn't coming in to drink but just to hang out, but
they used to card me anyway, especially at this one club called
The Tiger. They wouldn't let me in for nothing even though all
my friends were in there. "Okay," I said. "You're right. That's
the rules." Then, as soon as I turned 18 and had a reputation
as an All-American, they begged me to come in and just hang
out. "Sorry," I said. "Can't do it."

Maybe the team meeting helped, or maybe it was just because I was so much older and wiser as a 21-year-old, but we
really stomped the Clippers the next night 112–95. I took it to
Stanley Roberts pretty good again and must've gotten into his
head because he looked like me at the free throw line, missing
all four of his shots pretty badly. He finally fouled out. Jeff
Turner got tossed again for fighting, this time taking Ken Norman with him. The man is taking his Knucklehead status very
seriously.

One other thing: My friend Holly Robinson sang the national
anthem beautifully before the game. It was a huge coincidence
that she happened to be in town right around my birthday.
(Actually, she was there to do an appearance for Disney.)

We played the Knicks the next night and Robert Earl wanted
to celebrate my birthday at Planet Hollywood in New York. So
a bunch of us went over that afternoon and met Ah-nold.
There's only one Ah-nold. Ah-nold told me he wanted to put
me in his next "Terminator" movie, and I said I'd do it as long
as I could beat him up. He laughed. I think. I got an autographed picture from him and he came across as a really nice
guy. He's a lot shorter than he looks in his movies, though. But
when you make as much money as he makes, you can be any
height you want.

I don't know what it was with us and the Knicks all season, but we really had a war going. The Knicks won this one 109–107 in another overtime game. I fouled out with fifteen seconds left when I was called for knocking over Doc Rivers when he set a pick. Now that foul, in my opinion, was really ridiculous, the kind that shouldn't be called at any time, but certainly not with the game up for grabs down the stretch. I was as mad as I had been all season but the only thing I said was: "Next year that foul will go to Jamal Mashburn."

What I really want to say is this: Glenn Rivers, don't flop on me like that next time. Because if you do, I'm going to break your jaw. That's the penalty for flopping on that kind of play late in the game. Jaw-breaking.

I'll give Patrick the credit this time, though. He got 37 on me, although it took him 35 shots to do it. My shot wasn't falling. I made only 8 of 23, but, the funny thing was, I was really stroking my free throws and made 7 out of 8. Strange, strange game.

Before our next game, at home against Indiana, I had to go through a really bizarre interview with some film crew from England. The questions they asked me made me wish for those road trip interviews when I usually knew exactly what was coming. The main reporter was a nice-looking young lady in a miniskirt. I guess that's good journalistic strategy, figuring that I'd have to answer everything she asked me. But it was stuff like "What's your wardrobe?" and "Did Robin Givens really try to seduce you?" (The answer to the first question is "casual." The answer to the second is "no.") I cut 'em real short and they were mad because they had a long flight over. That wasn't my problem. I told Alex Martins: "No more interviews with people with funny accents." We won the game anyway, 119–106.

Around this time the Magic players had one of their mandatory Stay in School programs. Under the terms of the basic player agreement, we all have to make at least twelve appearances, six as an individual, six as part of a team. One of the

Magic's main team appearances is the Stay in School program, which the NBA is really behind. I was a little hesitant about it at first because I'm known for not staying in school. I came out of LSU early to go to the NBA, and I didn't want to look like a hypocrite. But when I found out that it was to help kids get their high school diploma, which is something I definitely agree with, I said okay.

The problem with it was that it was corny. I had gone to the first one and didn't like it. It was just, "Okay now, what does M stand for?" And they'd say "motivation." We'd spell out all the letters in M-A-G-I-C and they all meant something. It reminded me of when I was a kid and we had speakers come to school and they were usually boring. I didn't want to be the boring speaker that nobody listened to. So D. Scott and I got the idea to rap to them. We came in with the beat, got 'em dancing, then did our rap, then fit the whole thing into a stay-in-school message at the end. I bet it was the most successful jam they ever had.

One thing about me is that I don't like to be told what to do. (That's why I'm a Knucklehead.) That doesn't mean I won't listen, like if the coach knows something about basketball that I don't know. But if there's a better way to do something that comes from inside of me, then that's the way I want to do it. My point isn't that every single player in the NBA should rap. But guys are sometimes afraid to be creative, put some of themselves into their message. Maybe somebody knows card tricks. Maybe somebody else tells jokes. Maybe somebody else sings. But kids know when you're being real or not, and they're gonna listen closer to someone who's sincere. That's how I see it anyway.

I made a bad error before our game against the Hawks in Atlanta on March 12. After shootaround on the morning of the game I was heading back for my cheeseburgers and nap when a couple guys came by and asked me to go shopping. I thought I could make it back to get an hour or two of rest, but the mall was ten miles away and we got caught in a traffic jam and barely made the bus to the game. It upset my rhythm and we lost 110–92. Of course, it didn't help us either that Dominique was back healthy and scored 35.

The shopping trip was a success, though. I went to this hat store and bought one of those Mad Hatter hats like the dude wore in *Alice in Wonderland,* a huge black and white checkered lid. I have a thing for hats. I've got a Sherlock Holmes hat and all kinds of other ones. When I was in high school I used to walk around wearing a big coonskin cap, one of those Davey Crockett things on my head, along with a giant watch around my neck. One of my teachers, Mr. Jordan, used to just bust out laughing as soon as he laid eyes on me.

Speaking of laughing, nobody was doing much of it on the way home. We got caught in a lot of turbulence and couldn't land in Orlando. We tried Tampa and finally set down in Miami at about 3:30 A.M. There were wind gusts as high as seventy mph and, finally, lightning hit a transformer and put out the lights in the commuter terminal where we were waiting. By the time we got another flight and landed back home, it was 8 A.M. Another glamorous night in the NBA.

I never felt like we were in real danger or anything because the plane was just shaking from side to side. Shaking is okay. Going down full-speed is not okay. I hate to reveal team secrets, but my man, Greg Kite, probably looked the worst. Greg was just looking out the window, hanging on to the seat real tight, and looking a little whiter than usual. No doubt about it, the Big Bruiser was scared.

Shawn Kemp and I had a pretty good battle the next night. He had 27 points and 12 rebounds and I had 29 and 8 with 4 blocked shots. The Sonics beat us 105–97. I thought then that they were one of the best teams in the league and it didn't surprise me later when they made it to the Western finals.

The next day we left for a six-day trip West—three games in Texas, one in Denver. Obviously, it was going to be special because I was going back to San Antonio for the first time as a pro.

The trip got off to a bad start when the Rockets beat us 94–93 on a three-point shot late in the game by Robert Horry, a rookie. I had played against Robert for three years in college—he went to Alabama—and I can tell you that he never hit a shot from that far out in his life. But I like him as a player. He's 6'7", can run, jump, has handles, one of those guys who's going to be a lot better in the pros than he was in college. Of course, that's true of anyone who went to Alabama. They have a real crazy system down there, too many scorers, too many people fighting each other to get shots.

Hakeem and I had a good battle. He got more points, 20–16, and I got more rebounds, 17–15. But they just killed us with second and third shots, especially after we had a 17-point lead in the third period. A tough, tough loss.

But not as tough as the next night when we got beat by the Mavericks 102–96. To make matters worse, Scott Skiles separated his shoulder and missed the next four games. They were playing with desperation because, if they had lost, they would've tied the NBA record of twenty losses in a row. But desperation didn't have nothing to do with it.

I wouldn't be honest if I didn't tell you that this was one of these games where I honestly felt my teammates just didn't want me to excel. It was a known fact that Dallas had no inside game. Even teams without a scoring center dumped the ball inside on them. And I was killing them in the first half, dunking sideways, backwards, and scoring 20 points. But in the second half I almost never touched the ball. Guys were coming down and shooting twenty-foot jumpers, three-pointers, and we were playing absolutely no defense. We made them look like all-stars. Their point guard Morlon Wiley? We made him look like Kevin Johnson and John Stockton all rolled into one. Donald Hodge? Looked like Hakeem Olajuwon. Shaq? Looked like he wasn't in the game.

I'm not just imagining this. I went through fifteen minutes of the third and fourth period without trying a shot and had only three in the whole second half. One reporter wrote that a police artist should've given Matty Goukas a sketch of me so he would've recognized me. But Matty can't go out on the floor and *make* people pass me the ball. I finished with 21 and 12, but, I'm telling you, that was one game we should not have lost. My mom was there and even she said, "They didn't get you the ball enough."

Moms always know best.

And then it was time to go to San Antonio.

• • •

San Antonio was where I first made my mark in the basketball world. It was all struggles up until then. Struggles to keep me from acting up when I was young, struggles to get my skills on a par with my body all the time I was in Germany. But when we came back into the country and settled in San Antonio in April 1987, right after my fifteenth birthday, everything started to go right. It probably would've happened anyway. But it happened in San Antonio.

I completed my first two years of high school in Germany so I came back ready to start my junior year. The first thing I had to do was pick a high school, and, as I already told you, that was simple. My dad said: "You're going to this one." He didn't put no stock in those big 5-A high schools, and thought little ol' Robert C. Cole Junior and Senior High School was just fine.

It was small, a 2-A school, and there were a lot of kids coming and going because they were basically the sons and daughters of service people or what we called DOD civilians, Department of Defense employees. So, it wasn't anything strange when a black kid who had spent several years in Germany suddenly showed up in September. Of course, when a seven-foot black kid showed up, that was cause for some curiosity.

Texas is football country and San Antonio is no exception. Naturally, the football coach, a good guy named Joel Smith, wanted to know if I was interested. He had seen me throw a football seventy yards in the air and he imagined that more than a few tacklers might back away from a guy my size. But I told him about the aching in my knees every time I got chopped when I used to be a tailback and he never really bugged me about it anymore. Besides, Coach Smith was also the athletic director, so, unlike a lot of football coaches, he was also concerned about basketball. He figured he'd be better off saving me for that.

I did keep football stats for him for both of my years, though, sitting right there on the bench in the rain and the heat. We both figured that was a good psychological weapon. The other team would show up, and they'd introduce me, and they'd say, "Man, that kid's the statistician? How big are the players?"

I tell you, I loved that school. I have flashbacks of how much fun it was every time I go back to visit. A part of me will always remember it. In industrial shop class I made a wooden cutting board for my mother that said LUCILLE'S KITCHEN on it. She still has it hanging up. Everybody knew me because of my size and the fact that our basketball team was the best in the state, but I never asked for any special privileges and I never got any. There was a feeling at that school that I miss sometimes, the closeness between the coaches and the players, and the teachers and the students. By this time in my life I had pretty much learned how to have a good time without being a complete juvenile delinquent, and I got good grades in high school, mostly A's and B's, rarely a C or D.

And I had fun. Whenever I'd drive to school I'd always go park in Coach Smith's spot just to drive him crazy. I do the same thing now when I go home to visit. Mr. Jordan's history class was in a portable building and I used to be able to reach onto the roof, scoop up the gravel, and toss it on kids every once in a while, and that used to drive him crazy. I always told Mr. Jordan he could be my agent when I was ready to go pro, and when I went back there for a visit after announcing I was leaving LSU, he said, "Hey, Shaq, I thought I was your agent!" And I told him: "Oh, didn't I tell you? I fired you."

One time, just for fun, I picked up the principal, Mr. Buddy Compton, and held him up over my head. The average student didn't do that.

The only time I got into trouble at Cole was when I punched out a kid for being disrespectful to a teacher. I know that sounds too good to be true, but it's a fact. You can have fun with people older than you without showing them disrespect, and this kid didn't know how to do it. He was a little bit better at it after I clocked him.

When I say basketball turned around for me in San Antonio, I don't mean I didn't have some adjustments. In fact, when I first got there, and even through some of my junior year, I was still kind of a soft player. I still couldn't get that mentality to turn around and try to rip the rim off. My model at the time was actually Dominique Wilkins because of the way he made you go, "Ooh, look at that!" But I shouldn't have been trying to be an "ooh, look at that!" type of player. I needed to be a "Whoa! Get the heck out of the way!" type of player.

A couple things happened to change me. Out on the playground one day, this guy was talking noise to me, all the time, all up and down the floor. And I suddenly realized that must've been the "book" on me: *Talk to Shaq. Get him rattled. He's really a soft player. He won't tear it up on you.* And, man, after that I just went off on this guy, dunking everything right and left. My problem was, how could I work myself up to this angry temperament every time I stepped on the court? See, with me, it wasn't a natural thing. But I learned how to do it. I learned how to get a killer instinct on the court and just be a good guy off it.

So, my message is: you can learn to be a killer on the court. In fact, you have to. You've got to train your mind to do it if it doesn't happen to you naturally.

In high school ball, I developed the killer instinct during my junior year when I just got frustrated by all the noncalls. I was one of the few players in America whose high school coach wanted me to dunk *more,* instead of less. I'd take the ball to the hole all soft, have four guys grab both my arms and get no call. So one day I realized that all those little misses when I got fouled would at least be two points if I dunked. I didn't have any control over whether or not they were going to call the foul, but I could control the field goals. And that's what I started doing.

Like a lot of good high school players, though, I was cocky. I remember the first time I saw a story in one of those basketball magazines that called me "the game's next great player." My head was so big I could barely fit it through the doors of the high school. It's just something you gotta learn as a young player, and it usually takes something bad to get the lesson across.

For me it happened near the end of my junior year. We were 32–0 going into the regional finals, just killin' everybody, and we went up against this team called Liberty Hill, whose biggest guy was 6'3". I was 6'11" or 7'0" by then, the baddest thing in the country, or so I thought. I did everything wrong for that game. First, I stayed out late the night before, not drinking or anything like that, but just late enough to be tired the next day. Then, when the game started, I got into foul trouble right away, unless you don't think getting called for a personal on the opening tip is right away. Sure, I thought some of them were bad calls. When I showed up down in San Antonio, there was an adjustment period for the referees same as anyone else. They had never seen a mobile seven-footer and every time they'd see my hand up by the rim, for example, they'd call goaltending. But bad calls are going to happen. Then, we still could've won the game, but I missed two free throws with five seconds left and we lost. I felt terrible, as terrible as I had ever felt about anything in my life up to that point.

The lesson was: you better take a team seriously enough not to be put into a position where you can lose because of a couple tweets of the whistle or a couple missed free throws. I had other games when I missed two free throws and other games when I was in foul trouble, but, by concentrating the whole game, keeping that killer mentality about me, we were ahead by thirty points and it didn't matter.

What made it worse was, Liberty Hills was one of those teams that made a lot of racial remarks. Things got so ugly before the game that they had to stop the warmups. I think the refs were a little overwhelmed when the game started, and they stayed that way. The next year, in fact, when we played Liberty Hills again, they brought refs in all the way from Austin. It didn't matter. We killed them so bad that their fathers could've been reffing and it wouldn't have made a difference.

It was in the summer between my junior and senior year, 1988, that I got the most confidence. I played in the BCI tournament, the Basketball Congress Invitational in Houston, against guys who were supposed to be the best players in the nation and I dominated. I remember before one game I had an argument with my father and that just psyched me up to play against this guy named Matt Wenstrom, who was a 'footer from Houston, a huge guy who weighed more than I did. He was rated the best center in the nation, and, man, I just killed him. In a tournament in Arizona I went up against this gangly kid from Utah, 7'4", (now 7'6"), who I later found out was Shawn Bradley, who just became the second pick in the 1993 NBA draft by Philadelphia. Now, that was a little tougher at first. (Remember what I said about Manute and telephone poles?) He caught my first few shots because they were soft fallaways, but I finally got that killer mentality and started talking it to him.

And when I got home from that tournament—presto!—like magic there were suddenly all these letters and brochures from all kinds of colleges. I didn't know what happened. "Mom," I said, "how many places did you write to?" And she said, "I didn't do anything, son. They just arrived."

It was like that line in *Field of Dreams:* If you get it done, if you dunk on someone's head, they will come. Or something like that.

My confidence, not my cockiness, really grew during my

senior year. We had a great, great team, one of those teams when all the players complemented each other perfectly. If they collapsed on me, we had outside shooters to knock down the jumper. If the other team had a really good guard, we had a defender to stop him, or, at least, direct him my way. In one game I had twenty-two blocked shots. Nobody wanted to play us, not even the 5-A schools.

One of our real rivals was Randolph High School, which is mostly Air Force kids. They were an all-white high school fond of making racial remarks. A lot of stuff like, "Send them back to Africa" or "Make the African eat the ball." (I wonder if white people ever shout at each other, "Send him back to England.") Anyway, their best player was a big guy named David Johnson and the newspapers played it up that Shaq was finally going to get taken down by the big, bad white guy.

I swear I'm not making this up. By the second period, Dave Johnson was out of the game, on the bench, crying, emotionally distraught.

Another time we were playing this school that had just built a brand-new gymnasium that they seemed to think automatically turned them into the Lakers. All we heard about was this great new gym, and how they were going to upset Cole to celebrate the debut, and all this noise. And before the game Mr. Madura, our head coach, says: "Look, I don't care who gets the tap, get the ball back to Shaq, and, Shaq, I want you to dunk so hard you tear that thing off the backboard." Coach Madura was a conservative guy, but he just got tired of hearing about that new gym. Sure enough, we got the tap, back to me, fast break, slam, and I bent that brand-new rim down by about a foot. You could hear a pin drop in that brand-new gymnasium. They didn't have breakaway rims in those days and we played the whole game with the rim at that height. We won by about thirty.

This time, after 35 wins, we didn't stop. We got 36 in the state championship game. So my high school career ended with 68 wins, one loss.

• • •

The real fairy-tale ending would be that I came back to San Antonio and ripped David Robinson for about forty points. It didn't happen that way. But it wasn't as bad a trip as some people thought. For one thing, I got to spend some time at home. My dad whipped up some of his real pit barbecue which he's got right outside the house. The man knows his sauce. And my mom cooked my pregame meal. I was well fed if nothing else.

The problem was, we weren't playing real well at the time. We were out of sorts, out of synch. We had those two tough losses in Houston and Dallas. And, then, in practice at San Antonio, Brian Williams got involved in a couple disagreements with the coaches and, when Scott Skiles and Jeff Turner stepped in, he got into disagreements with them. Brian's got to chill once in a while, stop acting goofy and talking back to the coaches and maybe he'd get more PT. He's a real talented player who could really help us.

My parents had paid for about two hundred tickets and I had a lot of friends from high school there. I thought I'd get a warm reception, but there were a lot of boos, which I can't figure out. What did I ever do to San Antonio? I told you I don't really think of it as my home, but, for a while, it was my home, and I have some real fond memories from there. Maybe they knew that I was coming in to try to kill David, just like he'd be trying to kill me in Orlando. They couldn't blame me for that, could they?

Anyway, this one prominent referee whose name I won't mention since I'll be seeing him again and again, was just killing me with everything. Traveling. Three seconds. Touch foul. In the fourth quarter Antoine Carr, the Spurs' big power forward, got the ball, took it to the hole, and just plowed me over. I fell. I didn't flop. I fell. No call. So next time down I made a strong move, David fell down, and the ref called me for an offensive foul. By this time I'm just laughing it's so ridiculous. Next play they take a shot, miss, and I'm running down the court, trying to beat David, and they call an offensive foul on me. *While I'm running!*

So I say something to the official and get a technical. Now, I'm really angry, I admit it, and say: "Those calls were a bunch of b.s. and you know it!" So I get my second T and I'm gone, automatic ejection, still 6:45 left in the game.

Players make mistakes and coaches make mistakes, so referees can make mistakes. But the one thing a referee should not do is let his ego get in the way of a game. And referees do that all the time. In this situation they were determined to "keep the rookie in line" or something like that. I thought it was wrong, and I'll continue to think it's wrong as long as I'm playing. We lost 96–93.

But we came back to beat the Nuggets, 114–108. That showed I wasn't "devastated" by the game at San Antonio, like someone said. Disappointed, yes. Devastated, no. It's not in my personality to be devastated unless something happened to a loved one.

I'll be back to San Antonio. Unless I'm mistaken, the Spurs are on the schedule every year.

CHAPTER ELEVEN

Rewarding
Laimbeer

We came back from the trip and beat Miami at home, 103–89. I had what I call a real economical game, making most of my shots (13 of 18) and finishing with 28 points. I had 10 rebounds, too, and best of all only one turnover. More and more as the season went on, I was able to really let the game come to me, see the double teams, remain calm, know when to shoot it, know when to give it up. Obviously, that's the thing I have to get better at doing, along with free-throw shooting. But in this game everything was working. I shot jump *shots*, bro, not just jumpers, four of them in the second half that helped us pull away. After the game, Grant Long of the Heat said, "Shaquille was taking the shots we wanted him to take." Okay, I'll accept that. But after a few years there won't be any shots anybody will want me to take.

When I first got into the NBA I didn't think much about rivalries with individual teams. That seemed like the kind of thing you left behind in college. The Miami Heat didn't mean anything to me the first couple times we played them. But, gradually, that rivalry did become important. Everyone was always talking about being the best team in the state of Florida, and being a better expansion team than the Heat, and I started to get into it, too. Now, I want to beat those guys as bad as I want to beat anyone.

It was around this time that I filmed the Pepsi commercials. We had finally signed the Pepsi deal in February after months and months of publicity. We had actually gotten our first offer from a soft drink company way back in the summer, from 7-Up, which offered good money to do two commercials. But it would've canceled out both Pepsi and Coke so we said no.

Leonard was talking to both companies all the time, but it was taking Coke a real long time to make an offer. They have more committees over there than the U.S. government. Pepsi was real interested and made a presentation to me in Orlando early in the season and said they wanted me to be the spokesman for Mountain Dew. It didn't make either Leonard or me very thrilled. I kept having that "Ya-hoo! It's Mountain Dew!" line running through my head. I guess that means it was successful advertising since people remember it, but I looked on it as kind of a hillbilly thing and said I didn't want to do it. Leonard and I viewed Pepsi as the flagship brand and a more natural association for me, especially at first.

The way Leonard and I work is that I look at everything. Not every detail, but especially the lines I have to say or the slogans that are going to appear next to my name. It's getting back to what I said when I rapped at the Stay in School Jam instead of just reading the lines they handed me, or like getting directly involved in the charities instead of just putting my name on the letterhead. I don't want anything wack, anything corny to be approved that I don't know about.

Eventually, we got the deal done with Pepsi and I think both sides were really happy with the contract. Later in the year during the playoffs, Reebok and Pepsi were able to "piggyback" on my commercial, figuring that one would help sell the other. Signing with Pepsi kept me from making a possible deal with McDonald's because they're affiliated with Coke. But McDonald's still wanted to cash in on some of that Shaq popularity so they issued trading cards with me, Michael Jordan, and some other NBA stars on them. But before they could make it into the McDonald's stores, all the ones with Jordan and me started to disappear. It turned out that the district managers were stealing them and trying to sell them, and a bunch of employees landed up getting fired.

The filming for the Pepsi spots was completely different than it was for Reebok—so much easier, so much less hassle. I know kids are supposed to be hard to work with, but the ones in the Pepsi commercial were unbelievable, easier than most adults. I had had the script for a couple months before we actually shot, and I could tell right away there was nothing wack about it. Everything seemed real natural, like that one kid's line, "Don't even think about it." The guy who wrote it, Joe Pytka, is real famous in the business, the same guy that wrote the McDonald's ad for Jordan and Bird: "Off the scoreboard, over the second rafter, nothing but net." I didn't really add a thing except at the end when I look over at the camera with that real hopeless expression after the little kid turns me down for a sip. I think that's the one thing that sets me apart from the other athletes doing commercials—my facial expressions. I'm not a brilliant actor, but I think I have a feel for when a certain expression will tell a lot of the story.

After this shoot, I had a new name for myself: One-Take Shaq. Everything went smoothly, partly because of the script, partly because of the great kids, partly because I was a little more experienced at it. Working with the kids was great. I found out that one of the kids in the crowd scene was homeless. A lady from the shelter had set it up so he could come down there and make $400 to give to his mother. I told Dennis to go buy him a bike. So he went out and bought the kid a real nice bike and came back with it before we were done filming. Sometimes I wish I could do that for every homeless kid in America.

Both the Reebok and Pepsi commercials were great in their own way. They're targeted to two different audiences obviously, the Pepsi spot being like that famous Mean Joe Greene commercial for Coke, when he tosses the kid his jersey. I remember watching that when I was a kid and thinking what a great commercial it was. I don't think the Pepsi spot will be as well remembered as that, but I hope years from now somebody remembers it and it brings a smile to their face.

Nick Anderson and I brought a smile to his little boy's face a couple days later in Chicago where we played the Bulls on March 26. We went a day early and stopped over to see Joshua on his third birthday. Joshua lives in Chicago with his mom, and every time Nick sees him he asks, "Where's Shaq?" I gave him a $100 bill, and wrote on it, "Dear Joshua, happy third birthday, Shaq." He got a kick out of it.

The Bulls beat us 107–86. I had 12 points in the first quarter, but didn't get the ball much after that and finished with only 20 points on 11 shots. It was a strange game that way. Nobody had over 20 points, and Michael had only 18 points, which he can usually get with both hands tied behind his back. Before the game, Michael and I thanked each other for signing photos that we had exchanged, and I also informed Pippen that he had been officially named a Knucklehead.

I said it then and I say it now: The Chicago Bulls were the best team in the league last season. I knew it, everybody knew it. The Suns might've won more games, and the Knicks might've beat them out in the East, but nobody was surprised when the Bulls won it all because they have Michael Jordan and Scottie Pippen.

We came back home and beat the Nets 98–84 with Greg Kite and I playing a lot together as twin towers. The Big Bruiser even heard the crowd shout his name a couple of times, "Kite, Kite." That was real nice. Derrick Coleman was kind of quiet. He had 16 points and 10 rebounds. I had 27 and 17 and even got five steals, which was a career high for me. The best center in the NBA at getting steals is Hakeem. He's almost like a guard. You can't put the ball anywhere near him or he'll get it, plus he's able to dart around you and steal entry passes. I've got a long way to go to catch him in that department.

And then, on March 30, in came the Pistons. As I said, I liked and respected a few guys on that team. Isiah Thomas had been real nice to me at the All-Star Game. Joe Dumars is a great, great player, and a real quiet guy. Rodman is a Knucklehead. But when you get out on the court with them, you just want to beat them so bad you can taste it. And that's how bad they want to beat you. The Magic hadn't been very good at it, though. We had lost fourteen in a row over four seasons to them and we were determined that this game was going to be different.

We went after them from the beginning. We led 8–0, held them to just 13 points in the first quarter, and led by as many as 18 in the second period. They made the game hard for me, though. They were running an extra player or two at me every time I touched the ball and, when I did go to the basket, they were grabbing me, chopping me, pounding me. I was trying to just make the simple pass out of the double-team but it was still frustrating to have only 7 points going into the fourth period. There had been only one other game all year, on December 1 in Seattle when I had 9 points, that I didn't hit double figures.

The game was real intense. We were both fighting for a playoff spot and it showed. Laimbeer and I had words with about 3:40 left in the game because I got tired of him just hanging on me. Earlier he had chopped me in the head and I had just gotten tired of it. With 2:52 left Isiah got ejected for getting back-to-back technical fouls for arguing a personal foul call against Alvin Robertson. You should never argue a foul against Robertson because, the way he plays, it probably was a foul. Things were hot and heavy. You think the Pistons weren't fouling? We scored our last 19 points of the game from the line.

Then, with 2:13 left, they threw the ball into me and Laimbeer just wrapped me up. Didn't try to defend me, didn't try to do anything within the rules to stop me, just wrapped me up in some damn bearhug. I've been playing basketball for about sixteen years now and I just don't remember any of my coaches telling me about the bearhug defense. Even if you're slow and over the hill and have no feet left, in other words, if you're somebody like Laimbeer, you're still supposed to at least try to play defense.

Grabbing a guy around the waist to put him at the foul line instead of letting him try to dunk is an accepted thing in the NBA. Well, I'll tell you how I feel about that. When I was in high school, I saw a dude grab a guy and try to hold him, and the guy fell right on his butt bone and was paralyzed for a while. I have a phobia about someone grabbing me. It's not basketball, it's sumo wrestling.

After he grabbed me, naturally, Laimbeer turned away because he didn't want a confrontation. He wouldn't want a confrontation with a Girl Scout. I started after him because I was mad, not to punch him but to just say, "That's it. Don't wrap me up anymore." And all of a sudden, Alvin Robertson come running up like some damn mother hen and grabbed me.

I said, "Alvin, get off me!" He said something with the word "rookie" in it and I felt him nudge me in the groin. I know everyone said later that they couldn't see the nudge in the groin, but I felt it. And he kept talking, kept yakking, kept hanging on to me, like he was just dying to get hit. And all the time the refs never stepped in. It's funny, but when I watched the clip later, the one guy who was there right away, right after Laimbeer grabbed me, was Scott Skiles, our smallest player. All these 6'8" and 6'9" guys around and there was Scott Skiles. Anyway, I just got my fill of Robertson pretty quickly, and it looked like he was going to keep talking and talking. So I clocked him—boom!—quick right hand to the face. And they ejected me. Fortunately, we held on to win 105–91. We shot 47 free throws and, believe me, it had nothing to do with being the home team. It could've been 147.

Did I feel bad about the ejection? Sure I did because they suspended me for the next game against Charlotte. Losing about $46,000, my game's pay plus the $10,000 fine, was the small part. I don't want to miss any game, much less one that I'm healthy for. My father was in the stands and I'm sorry he saw me lose my temper like that. But even after I've had time to think about it, I don't know if I'd do anything different the next time. There are differences between hard fouls and dirty fouls. Players like Laimbeer constantly cross the line. There are ways you put a guy on the free throw line and ways you don't, and players like Laimbeer do it the wrong way.

Look at how big I am, and I've never in my life committed a foul that I thought could deliberately hurt someone, or jolt him so bad that he could be paralyzed, which is what Laimbeer's bearhug does. I'm a shot-blocker, so I'm always going for the ball, always throwing my body in the air, and I could hurt any number of players. But the way I commit a hard foul is to give a guy a little body, jump into him a little bit, let him know I'm there, instead of going for the head or wrapping him up.

The big theory among the journalists after the game was that Laimbeer had "tricked" me into the fight. There wasn't any trickery about it. Eventually, you have to stand up for yourself. I told Laimbeer to stop fouling me deliberately, I warned him. If the referees can't step in and do something to stop those bearhugs, then this kind of thing is going to keep happening.

I'm almost always able to control my temper out on the court and that's one of the things that's really helped me in basketball. But people tend to remember fights that big seven-footers have. An aggressive little guy like Scott Skiles can have a dozen fights a year, but I guarantee that people will remember the one Shaq fight.

That's why, in some people's minds, my whole college career can be summed up when I got thrown out of the SEC tournament for fighting in my junior year. Either that, or they'll remember that LSU, my team, never went as far as it was supposed to. I'm going to tell you about all that. But I'm going to tell you about the good times, too, because there were a lot of them.

• • •

It wasn't a hard decision for me to go to LSU. Sure, Coach Brown had the in from the beginning because of our meeting in Germany way back before I could hardly dunk. But that wasn't the only reason.

I had four other schools besides LSU on my list—North Carolina, North Carolina State, Illinois, and Arizona. All the coaches came to see me, and I liked all of them. Dean Smith of North Carolina, Jim Valvano of North Carolina State, Lou Henson of Illinois, and Lute Olsen of Arizona. I can remember when Dean Smith visited Cole and lit a cigarette in the athletic director's office. Now, Coach Smith, that's Joel Smith, the football coach and athletic director at Cole, never let anyone smoke in there, but he made an exception for Dean. He always said it was the highlight of his life when Dean Smith came to visit him. I reminded him that the highlight of his life was supposed to be getting to hang out with me. So he moved Dean Smith down to second. Greg Carse, the LSU assistant, spent so much time at Cole recruiting me, even sleeping on the couch in the athletic office from time to time, that Coach Smith used to joke that he was going to charge him rent.

I liked LSU from the beginning. It was fairly close to San Antonio, first of all, so my parents could come see me play, even if they had to drive (which they landed up doing most of the time). I liked the hot weather—Illinois would've been tough for that reason—and I liked the conference, the SEC. I looked at it as a big, tough, roughneck, countryboy conference, not like the ACC which was kind of the pretty, rich-boy conference. I felt comfortable there, and I signed early, in

November of my senior year, just so my family and I wouldn't be hassled with phone calls all year. My dad went out and got an LSU flag and hung it above our front door in San Antonio, just like he put an Orlando Magic flag up there a few years later.

And whether or not you believe it, I never got one single thing to go to LSU. I have nothing to hide now, and I'd tell you if it happened. In one of the first conversations Dale Brown ever had with my family, my father told him: "The first person who offers us something illegally or under the table is going to get kicked out of our house on his butt." In fact, Coach Brown always said that no family he ever dealt with was more concerned about NCAA rules than us. One time, while I was at LSU, a friend of my father's wanted to take me out to dinner. I even checked with Coach Brown on that because I didn't want to see no headlines that said: SHAQ ON THE TAKE. Even when reporters came down to do a story on me I insisted on paying for my own sandwich when I'd take them over to Blimpie or Subway.

I went down to LSU in the summer before my freshman year to take a job at an industrial construction company outside of Baton Rouge. On my first day on the job I'm out in the middle of this field someplace and a big, old tornado came whipping through the site.

"Uh, oh," I told one of my co-workers. "I'm outta here."

"Don't worry about it," he said.

It turned out to be Dennis Tracey. That's where our friendship began. He always remembers the day I arrived in Baton Rouge. I brought a tornado with me.

I'd be lying if I said the basketball part at LSU worked out for me as well as I hoped. Every high school star wants to go to college, get on TV a lot, play against All-Americans, make the Final Four. I did all those things except make the Final Four. Our best year, everybody thought, was my freshman year, when we were ranked No. 2 in the country for a while. Chris Jackson was already there, and Stanley Roberts was going to be playing after sitting out his freshman year because of grades. I knew about Stanley and a lot of people wanted to know why I'd go to a school where they had another 'footer. I don't worry about stuff like that. And, anyway, it wouldn't have made any difference if Stanley was seven feet tall or five feet tall—he was hard to play with, a little lazy, a little unmotivated. And Chris Jackson had a lot of talent but he didn't like to give up the ball.

That didn't matter at first because I came in willing to play only defense my freshman year. In fact, Coach Brown always had to holler at me to shoot more. But when I look back, maybe I should've been more of an offensive player and taken over games instead of leaving it to Chris all the time. At times we played up to our talent. We beat UNLV, which went on to win the NCAA championship, 107–105. We outscored Loyola Marymount 148–141 in overtime. What I remember about that game was blocking Hank Gathers's first seven or eight shots (I finished with 12 blocks altogether) and the man *still* got 40 on us. Talk about somebody with a scorer's mentality. It was sad, really sad, when he died.

We came into the SEC tournament with a 24–7 record but lost in the first round to Auburn 78–76, a team we had beaten easily two times before. We had been up by twenty points and just completely blew it. After the game, Coach Brown was screaming, "Will anybody stand up and lead this team? Doesn't anybody want to take charge?" Dennis Tracey looked over at me and I knew what he was thinking: Stand up, Shaq, please stand up. But I was a freshman, and I just didn't think it was my place.

We won our first-round NCAA game against Villanova, but then we lost to Georgia Tech, which had Dennis Scott, Kenny Anderson, and Brian Oliver, by three points, 94–91. The regional final was in New Orleans that year, 60 miles from LSU, and it would've been great to make it there and then to the Final Four. But it wasn't meant to be.

I learned a big, big lesson from that team. We had all that

talent and yet we lost nine games. The next year, Chris went to the NBA, Stanley went to Europe (it had nothing to do with me; going to class just wasn't in Stanley's plans), and everybody said we'd be a real mediocre team. Georgia, Alabama, and Kentucky were all supposed to be better than us. But we won the SEC. We had one All-American, me, one should've-been-All-American, Vernel Singleton, and a bunch of role players like Justin Anderson, Mike Hansen, Shawn Griggs, and T. J. Pugh. But we played together. We had chemistry. Everyone wasn't looking out for himself.

Maybe my favorite college game happened during that year, the Arizona game in December. It was on national television and Dick Vitale came down to the locker room and talked to me before the game. I had met him the first time at the McDonald's All-American High School game when he almost had a heart attack on the air describing how I went coast-to-coast and dunked. "Shaq," he said, "I don't think you can beat these guys, but do your best." I love that kind of talk. I got our guys in the huddle and said, "Everybody thinks we're gonna lose. Let's go out and play hard and show them different." Arizona was the No. 2 team in the nation then, and they had a front line that everybody was calling the Tucson Skyline, with my future Magic teammate Brian Williams, Sean Rooks, and Chris Mills.

I was actually having a mediocre game when I happened to catch my mom's eye with about six minutes to go. I saw her mouth the words, "Take over." And that's what I did. From that point on, I scored 16 points (to finish with 29), got about 10 of my 14 rebounds, and we won 92–82. Somebody played me the tape of Dick Vitale later and again, it sounded like he was having a heart attack describing my performance. Dick, I'm glad you stopped down before the game, bro.

During my final home game that season, the student cheering section shouted, "Two more years!" every time I made a dunk or something. After the season, as I told you before, I did think briefly about the NBA, but I didn't have any good reason to go except for money. So there was really no question I was coming back, and, at the time, I had no reason to believe it wasn't for two more years.

I think we could've surprised some people and won the SEC tournament, too, except that I suffered a hairline fracture of the left leg late in the season. They thought it was just a bad bruise at first and I missed the last game of the regular season. But then the X-rays came back showing the fracture, and I missed our opening tournament game against Auburn. We lost 92–77. Those were the only two games I missed during my college career.

My junior year was more bad chemistry, too many egos, too much what's-in-it-for-me? thinking. I had to put a couple people in check on that team, especially Jamie Brandon, a point guard who somehow had the idea he was the main man. But I'll admit that even I started out slow and I'm not sure why. In the first game of the year Northeast Louisiana had three guys on me all the time, and I only had 15 points and 15 rebounds. When teams discovered they could do that, we were doomed, so maybe that set the tone for the season. My grandmother, Odessa, even called me up from New Jersey and got on my case about how bad I was playing. "You're playing weak," she told me. And then the stories started coming out about how Mourning and Laettner were going to be the top picks in the draft and how Shaq was slipping. That's when I turned it on, stopped helping guys up and slapping them on the butt and shaking their hand.

And we did have some good games that year. We put a 159–86 hurtin' on Northern Arizona. They had a center named David Wolfe who said before the game, "I'm gonna huff and puff and blow the Shaq down." The Shaq had 43 points, 19 rebounds, and 8 blocked shots on the big, bad Wolfe. We beat Kentucky, the team that almost went to the Final Four except for Christian Laettner's famous shot, by twenty points. What I remember about that game was how they would not come inside at all to challenge me. They took forty-four three-point shots and made only eight of them. In a nonconference game against McNeese State, I was running down the lane trailing a fast break when I took a missed shot, windmill-dunked it and at the same time jumped completely over a 6'5" guy named Melvin Johnson. Down in Baton Rouge they still just call that The Dunk.

But all in all it wasn't fun. The team wasn't close, and I had three and four defenders hanging on me every play. Coach Brown used to say that people were getting arrested out on the street for doing what they did to me on a basketball court. He even made a tape of cheap shots and fouls that weren't called on me and sent it to the SEC office.

But I tried to control my temper. I got technicals from time to time, sure. One time I slammed the ball down real hard at Kentucky and got one. But I didn't get into fights. Dennis used to tell me that I should let it out and maybe it would be better if I went and hit a punching bag or something. But I thought that was silly.

Then came the Tennessee game in the SEC tournament in Birmingham. They had this big roughneck guy, Carlos Groves, who couldn't do anything but foul and talk. Foul and talk. If they had a position for fouling and talking, he would've been All-American. We're ahead 51–33 at halftime and it's really no contest. So in the second half I'm all by myself ready to take a layup and he comes from behind and bearhugs me. Then he won't let go even when I come down. Man, that was it. I broke through his grip and, I'll admit it, I tried to go for his face with my elbow, but I didn't get him square. Neither of us ever threw a punch or even faced off like we were going to. He wanted no part of me in a fight.

But the next thing I knew, there were fights all over the place. I saw Coach Brown out there throwing a few haymakers. It was crazy. When I look back, I really don't think the incident with me and Groves would've been that big of a deal except for all the fights that followed. When Coach Brown got out there, it got really crazy. But I don't blame him. He was always an emotional coach, and he was out there protecting his player. So they threw me out of the game and later announced that I'd also be suspended for the remainder of the SEC tournament, which was a shame for the SEC tournament because a lot of people wanted to see the Jamal Mashburn-Shaq showdown in the next game. Actually, we played pretty well but Kentucky beat us 80–74. I watched the game from the stands. Before it started I was sitting on the LSU bench in streetclothes because nobody told me I couldn't. So they had to come down and tell me to move.

Everybody assumed that the Tennessee game was the one that convinced me to leave LSU and go into the NBA. But that isn't true. I don't think I spent nearly as much time thinking about the NBA as other people spent thinking about it for me. After the SEC tournament, I had only one thought in my mind: Get to the Final Four. Somehow. If I would've sat down by myself and thought it all out, yes, maybe, I would've said that this was my last year. But I didn't do that. I was thinking only of the Final Four.

We beat BYU in our first-round regional game 94–83. And then came Indiana. I've never been more ready to play a basketball game than I was that afternoon. And some people said it was the best college basketball game I ever played—36 points, 12 rebounds, 5 blocked shots, two steals, and, in case anybody forgets, 12 of 12 from the foul line, thank you very much. But we fell a little short, 89–79, and it was over. My reaction? I was pissed. I thought we had punked out against them. We had the lead in that game and played like we didn't want to win, missing a bunch of three-pointers in the last ten minutes. Everybody thought I was in the locker room thinking about my pro career but what I was thinking was, "I never made it to the Final Four." I put the NBA out of my mind, I really did.

I then came back to Baton Rouge for a few days, and, suddenly, around midnight one day, I just hopped in my car and started driving to San Antonio. And it was during that drive that I decided for sure that I was leaving college. I talked it over with my parents and they agreed. It was like all the decisions I ever made—once I made them, I didn't look back, didn't second-guess myself. I called up my academic counselor at LSU and dropped my courses. I called up Coach Brown and told him. I called a press conference at the youth center on the base in San Antonio and told everybody I was leaving. My parents, I'm sure, still wanted me to get my degree, but they stood behind me. It was silly to keep doing something that wasn't fun and wasn't helping me grow as a player.

It didn't have anything to do with Coach Brown, either. He's a nice guy, a good motivator, and I never had any problems with him. As the brothers on the street say, "I got no beef with him." I don't think he was the greatest coach in the world for my game, but that's the way it goes.

Anyway, the college game really isn't made for seven-foot centers. They can triple-team you, foul you intentionally, and the refs just don't have much sympathy. They say, "Hey, he can take it, because he's big," as if that should have anything to do with it. I don't think in the NFL they let guys clip Bruce Smith just because he's a big, tough defensive end. Rules are rules, or they're supposed to be. I remember one team and one team only that came out to single-team me from the beginning of the game—Arkansas State in my junior year. And I scored 53 on them. I'm not saying that would've happened to every team that single-covered me, but it's an indication.

When a team has a big center who gets a lot of media attention, that team is automatically supposed to win it all. And when it doesn't, it means that the center is a loser. But it just doesn't happen that way. Some big guys win it, some don't. How good was Hakeem Olajuwon at Houston and they got upset by North Carolina State? Hakeem never won. David Robinson never won it at Navy because his supporting cast wasn't nearly good enough. Patrick Ewing won it once, but look at Georgetown a few years later. They had Dikembe Mutombo and Alonzo Mourning, two guys who turned out to be good NBA centers, and they didn't get close to a national championship.

I had pressure and expectation my whole college career. One year the LSU sports information department counted that I was on the cover of nine preseason magazines. But I just dealt with it, letting that stuff go in one ear and come out the other. And to anyone who thought I had a "disappointing" college career, that's your problem, not mine.

Anyway, college was more than basketball, believe it or not. My first year I had a 2.9 grade point average, best on the basketball team. I always went to my study halls and arranged with the professors to make up work when I was away. People don't realize how tough it is to play basketball and stay on top of your work. Unlike football or baseball, basketball goes across both semesters and you're gone, sometimes, for a week at a time. But I kept up with it because I had to. I didn't like some of the things you had to take your first two years, like typing. I knew someday I'd be owning buildings, not typing in them. But I got through it.

I'm not going to pretend I was a Rhodes Scholar. I usually started out a semester with twenty-one or twenty-four hours and, if I was doing bad in a subject, maybe I would drop it. But I never got an F, and I never took bogus courses like basket-weaving and refrigerator maintenance. I took real courses, in business, accounting, and math. And if I would've stayed for my senior year, I would've graduated. Maybe I would've gone to summer school after my junior year, but I would've gotten that diploma.

I liked being a college student. I liked hanging out in the quadrangle on campus and talking to people. I never hid from anybody, was never unfriendly, tried to make people feel good. Coach Brown always said that what he remembers about me was not anything to do with basketball but how nice I always treated his wife, his daughter, and his grandchild. I appreciate that. I have good thoughts about LSU, nothing but good thoughts, in fact. But I'm not going to be one of these guys who just goes back and hangs around campus every spare moment to get standing ovations at the basketball games. College was then. This is now.

CHAPTER TWELVE

Another Basket Comes Down

I told the local newspapers that I had a date for the game that I was suspended for, after the Pistons game. So *The Orlando Sentinel* ran the headline: O'NEAL SPENDS EVENING WITH DATE. April Fools'. My only date for the evening was Dennis Tracey, and he doesn't count. I lounged around on the bed, watching the Charlotte game on TV, making a few phone calls, listening to some music, playing with the dog, trying to cheer on Greg Kite and Brian Williams to get after Alonzo Mourning.

The guys did all right. Kite even made the Knucklehead sign when he ran out for the starting lineup announcements. Brian had some good moments, too. But we lost 102–93 and Alonzo kind of went off on us with 30 points.

I spent about two minutes at the beginning of the game

feeling regrets, but it's not in my nature to worry about "ifs." The suspension happened, and we all had to deal with it. Players have been suspended in the past, players will be suspended again. Alex Martins wanted me to make an apology to the fans but I wouldn't do it. I really didn't think I had anything to apologize for. I wouldn't expect them to apologize to me if they booed me for some reason. I wouldn't expect them to thank me if I had a big game and helped us win. Fans are fans, players are players. The newspaper even ran a big poll: Did Shaq let the team down? About 1,000 voted yes, about 2,000 voted no.

But there's no doubt that fans are part of the life of an athlete. I told you that with our advance planning, Leonard, Dennis, and I were ready for almost everything that came our way, and I think Alex Martins and I were ready for almost all the publicity. But one thing we weren't ready for was the fan mail. Tons of it. Hundreds and hundreds of letters every week. I honestly don't know how many, but, by the end of the season, there were at least ten full boxes around the house. Dennis Tracey thinks the total was about one thousand pieces of mail per week.

I'm not going to lie to you: I don't read anywhere near all of it. That would be impossible. I could spend twenty-four hours a day reading fan mail and responding to it, but then I wouldn't have any time left to play basketball and I don't think the Magic would like that. They didn't pay me to read, they paid me to lead.

The toughest kinds of letters are the charity-related ones. You know, "Dear Shaq. We love you. You're great. You're wonderful. Please send us an autographed jersey for this, and a pair of autographed sneakers for that. Remember, we love you."

Now, is that fan mail? Or is it just somebody who wants something from you? If I would've sent an autographed jersey to everyone who asked me for one this year, I would've gone through a lifetime supply of jerseys for every player in the

league and then some. Is somebody who wants an autographed basketball card really a fan, or is he some dealer
trying to increase his profit? That's why it's impossible to send
autographed cards through the mail unless I really know the
person.

By the end of the 1992–1993 season, we had gotten the fan
mail situation pretty organized. We separated it into business
mail, charity mail, and personal. We put all the names and
addresses of the people we were going to answer on a database
and sent everyone the same thing, kind of a fan packet. Sure,
I think people were upset with us that we didn't get right back
to them, but this was like another fulltime job. Dennis was
already complaining that he was doing the work of six people
until I once again had to remind him that I had saved him from
a life of poverty. We finally got Jeff Ryan, who had run the
Shaq Pack at the arena, to help us out.

What I told Dennis was, I'd want to see at least a few pieces
of mail every week, usually something from a kid. If somebody
would send me a nice picture, or some classroom would mail
me a poem or something, we'd tack it up on the refrigerator.
Those are the kinds of things that interest me, not business
propositions, because kids are usually sincere. If there's a
whole group of people waiting for me after practice and it's
impossible to shake hands with all of them, I'll call down one
or two of the little kids because they're the ones who are
special.

Some of the letters will break your heart. I'll read them
and get so emotional that I'll just pick up the phone right
away and call the kid. I've done that a dozen times this year,
and, to me, it's better, more direct, more immediate, than a
letter. I'm from the reach-out-and-touch-someone generation, bro, which is why I carry a cellular phone around all
the time. One young woman wrote me and said that her
baby boy was in an Orlando hospital to get some kind of
special treatment. "If you can come by on Sunday, please
come by." So I stopped by and she couldn't believe it. I fol-

lowed up on it, too. Luckily, her son's going to be all right.

Here's an example of how sad these letters can be. (I changed the boy's name.)

> Dear Mr. O'Neal,
>   My best friend, John Doe, is dying of cancer. He is 13. You are John's favorite basketball player. He is working on a drawing of you shattering the backboard with a dunk. Basketball is his favorite sport, but he couldn't play last year or this year because of the cancer on his sciatic nerve. Would you please call John at the hospital? But, please, hurry.

Now, if that won't wreck your day, I don't know what will. I picked up the phone right away and made the call. But it's not always possible. I'd like to respond to every single letter like that but I can't always do it. Sometimes it doesn't get through to me. Sometimes I call and nobody's there and I just don't have time to call again. But I'm trying.

●   ●   ●

Immediately after watching the Charlotte game on TV, I drove to the arena and met the team for the flight to Indianapolis to play the Pacers. The next morning, D. Scott and I got up at 7 A.M. and drove out to the prison in Naperville where Mike Tyson was an inmate. Dennis Scott knew somebody who helped us get on the list because Mike was only allowed a few visitors per month. I didn't know him beforehand or anything, but he had always made a big impression on me, seeing this young kid just wrecking everybody. I always liked to watch him fight—you talk about someone with the killer mentality— and he knew about me, too.

I'm not going to violate him and tell you everything we talked about, but we were mostly just laughing and joking, and I think he appreciated the company. We were together for three hours. (In fact, we almost missed the shootaround at Market Square Arena.) I was impressed with him. I'm not going to get into what he did, or didn't do to get him in prison, but I was impressed with him as a man. And one thing I didn't like was when he told me that the guards really treated him bad, got a kick out of harassing him just because of who he is. You've got to be a strong man to endure that, and I think he's going to come out of prison as a mature person.

I don't care what kind of time you're doing, prison can't be fun. Fortunately, I've stayed out of trouble in my life so I don't have any firsthand experience. One time during my sophomore year I was driving between Baton Rouge and Shreveport and got picked up in this small town for speeding, and they took me to the courthouse and said I might have to spend a night in jail. It never happened, and I was happy about that.

A couple days after our visit, the Suns came to play the Pacers and Charles Barkley applied to see Tyson. He got turned down because Mike's visitor list was already full for the month.

Sorry, Charles.

After losing to the Pacers 118–102, we went to Miami. On our off night, April 3, Dennis and I went to eat in this restaurant in Coconut Grove that's also well known as an oldies place. There was a long-haired band on stage, real good guys, and they called Dennis and I up there. And all of a sudden, there we were singing, "Lou-I-Lou-I-A. Oh-oh. Lou-I-Lou-I-A." Then we went into, "Do-wah-diddy-diddy-dum-diddy-do. Do-wah-diddy-diddy-dum-diddy-do." I knew the song from *Stripes*, that Bill Murray movie where the army dudes sing it when they're marching. I must've seen that movie a million times. D. Scott and I knocked 'em dead, bro, even that University of Miami coach, Dennis Erickson, who was there. They loved us.

So did the Heat. They beat us 124–106. Unless we got hot again, the playoffs were going to start slipping away.

And right like that, we did turn it around. We're a young team, and a couple of times it did appear things were getting away from us. But we were usually able to regroup just when everybody thought we were going off the deep end. We had that real bad streak in the beginning of December when we lost six straight, and another five-game fade that included the Texas trip. But, besides those, we were always able to pick ourselves up after a couple of losses. That's a good sign for a young team that's still getting used to each other.

First we beat Philly 116–90. I had 22 in the first half, 35 for the game with 16 rebounds. After the game Nick said: "I don't think they wanted anything to do with Shaq," and that's the way it seemed to me, too. I had 13 dunks and shot only two free throws because they just weren't challenging me at all, never double-teaming or anything. I wish more teams had Philly's philosophy.

Then we won at Charlotte, 109–96, and I had a real good game against 'Zo—29 points, 10 rebounds. I'll say this for him in that game—he made all eleven of his free throws. I look down the road and I see an unbelievable rivalry among centers in the Eastern Conference. You've got Patrick at the top of his game in New York, you've got Alonzo, and you've got me, and that's not even to mention Brad Daugherty. So, when it comes to All Star time, it's going to be real close every year, one of those little voting battles that will really attract the fans.

'Zo's known for talking a little but he doesn't talk to me. He does talk to other players on our team. Once he dunked on Nick and he was pointing and stuff, but he doesn't do that to me. If he does, I'll talk back. I speak when I'm spoken to.

We weren't the only rivals in the game, though. When it was over, Kendall Gill ran after Scott Skiles and threw his gum at him. Scott's competitiveness can make other guys mad once in a while.

And then we went up to Minnesota and beat the Timber-wolves 95–92, a real satisfying game since all our starters scored in double figures. Nick's jump shot late in the game was the key hoop. I felt good because I was able to get Christian Laettner's shot four times. I finished with 29 points, 9 rebounds and 6 blocks. After the game a bunch of Viking players came in to shake my hand. I started to tell them about my career as a tailback but decided they wouldn't be impressed.

The Timberwolves have one of these big remote-control blimps that flies around the arena, and I'm thinking about getting one for my house. The arena people say they cost about $6,000. If I get one, I'm going to write "Shaq Daddy" on it. Even though I didn't buy the blimp, Minnesota was a great shopping trip for me. Not for clothes. That's not me. A lot of guys don't consider they've had a good trip unless they paid $1,000 for a leather jacket or something. I like toys.

Right across from the hotel was this martial arts store where I bought a ninja sword for $100. See, ninjas are important in my philosophy. To me, there are three different types of basketball players—good, great, and unstoppable. And there are three different types of martial arts people—tae kwan do, karate, and ninjas. And ninjas are like the unstoppable ones, the ones that do a lot of the unseen stuff, like they're quick, almost invisible. Sometimes I consider myself a ninja—running around, jumping high, coming down, slamming fast, doing things before people realize I'm doing them. Dennis and I have a ninja routine around the house. We'll sneak around, shout "ninja!" and pounce, maybe throw a pencil or leap out at the guy, like Peter Sellers and his crazy servant used to do in those Pink Panther movies.

Right now I don't do karate, but I might take it up someday as a form of self-defense. And if you drive by my house and see me swinging that ninja sword around, don't get worried. It's not very sharp and if I accidentally hit myself I won't get cut. It's just an ornament. When I move into a bigger house I'm going to have a ninja room with swords, ninja stars, and ninja masks. I bought one of those at the store, too, and wore it to the next couple home games. Ninja Shaq!

My favorite form of relaxation is to watch karate movies. It started a long time ago in Germany where there used to be Karate Matinee every Saturday morning at nine A.M. I like the moves. I love the parts where the Japanese people are talking and you see their mouths moving, but it's an American voice coming out. I like the clothes they wear, their style, their jumping ability, everything about them.

Then I went to this pet store and bought a $30 cookie jar that, when you open it, it barks. See, Dennis and I fight over food sometimes at home. He's always eating my cookies, but, after I got this, I could put all of them in this cookie jar, and, when I hear that bark, I know he's robbing it. Actually, it turned out to be more of a toy for Shazam. We open that jar and he goes crazy when he hears the barking, figuring that there's a dog hidden in there.

Minnesota was one of those places where the security was real bad, maybe because we only made one trip there all year. There were hundreds of people waiting when we went out to the bus and we were on a tight schedule. So I took the service elevator down, came around behind them, and slipped on the bus, my best backdoor move of the season. Sometimes you have to pull those ninja tricks.

Milwaukee was a bad experience all the way around. First, they were having a crisis with contaminated water and I couldn't even take a shower. We were actually allowed to but I like to stay in the shower a real long time, drinking in the water and spitting it out, and I knew I would forget not to do that. Then we lost the game 108–97 without Nick and Tom Tolbert, who were both hurt, Nick with a hamstring strain, Tom with a sprained left ankle. That left us one game behind Indiana for eighth place, the last playoff spot. I almost got into it with Milwaukee's center, Danny Schayes. We collided under the basket once, he went sprawling, and got up yelling at me. He's a hacker and a flopper, a candidate for a Laimbeer on Academy Awards night. So is Brad Lohaus. I was in foul trouble a lot of the game and played only thirty-three minutes.

After the game, the Bucks people grabbed me and asked me to sign some stuff for the team. Let me explain how this works. That happens in almost every city we go to. Alex tells me about it beforehand and, if it's reasonable, I'll do everything possible.

Our front office people get stuff signed from other teams, too. But in Milwaukee we heard nothing about it until they said, right as we were leaving, "Oh, Shaq, could you sign some stuff?" And we went into this room and counted 140 separate articles that they wanted autographed. That's crazy. And I walked out, the only time all year I didn't sign for another team. We were definitely glad to take our bottled water and get out of Milwaukee.

As Dennis Tracey and Alex Martins know, I'll do almost anything if it's reasonable and if I know about it. But I don't like surprises. I like surprises in my life but not in my schedule. When Dennis and I were first working things out way back in May 1992, even before the draft, we were in Louisiana one day and Dennis had a friend who wanted three basketballs autographed for a charity auction. We happened to be at a bank near the guy so Dennis, without telling me, called the guy up and told him to meet us at the bank with the basketballs. I was real nice to the guy, signed what he wanted, talked to him, said goodbye, then really went after Dennis when he left.

"If you ever, ever tell someone they can do something without asking me, I'm gonna be all over your case," I said.

And from then on, there weren't many surprises.

I didn't have enough time to put together too much for Easter, and they don't have many Easter bunny costumes for 'footers. But I did walk around the Arnold Palmer Hospital passing out baskets to the kids.

I officially declared the next day "Ninja Pig Hunting Day" and a bunch of us—Anthony Bowie, Brian Williams, Dennis Tracey, and me—went out to this hunting club near the airport to shoot boars and chase around these little piglets. I don't think there's anything in our contract prohibiting pig hunting but in a way it's worse than skiing considering the amount of cow dung we had to run through chasing these piglets. When we went deeper looking for boar, I got up on one but he spotted me and took off. Hard to sneak up on something, bro, when you're my size. Dennis shot a big one, though, about a

235-pounder. These hunters who took us went to Botswana over the summer and invited me to come with them. I'll probably do it someday. I always liked to shoot at targets and bowling pins and things like that. My dad, being in the army, was a pretty good shot.

But mostly the shots I'll be working on are fifteen-foot jumpers.

On the court, we kept hanging in there. On April 13 we beat the Bucks at home 110–91 to put our record at 37–38. Danny Schayes had to leave the game because of a scratched left eye he got when he tried to block one of my dunks. Jeez, and I had just run out of sympathy cards. D. Scott really turned into Triple D on that night. He made nine three-point shots to lead the way, including a thirty-nine-footer while tumbling backward to beat the shot clock. That's when you know you've got it going. Our lockers are right next to each other, and, after the game, the crowd wasn't around me for a change. D, I wish it happened more often.

We had an off game in Philly, losing 101–85, and right after the game we flew to Cleveland. I was real tired when I woke up the next morning and when I stepped out into the hallway the first thing I saw were two midgets. Now, I might see two midgets in ten years, so I figured I was still asleep. I went back into my room to regroup, came back out again, saw about a half dozen more lounging around the balcony and another half dozen on the elevator. It turned out there was what they called a Little People Convention going on at the hotel. I was not invited.

My first thought was, "Where do they get their clothes?" That's what a lot of people ask me, too. My answer is that I get them at my tailors, who are in L.A. and Atlanta. (I'm glad to have them. When I was in college I always looked like I shopped at the local welfare store because Baton Rouge was not exactly loaded with big men's shops.) So I wondered if there are tailors that specialize in clothes for little people, and if a little people suit would cost as much as one for me. See, I think it would. Dennis Tracey, who's about a foot shorter than me, gets some of his suits from my tailor and it drives him crazy that we pay the same price.

Anyway, the Cavs don't have many little people in their lineup, except for Mark Price. We had a real nice comeback from twenty-one points down but we lost 113–110. Scott Skiles had a three-pointer that just missed at the buzzer, and all of us believed we would've beaten them in overtime. The loss left us two games behind Indiana with five left. Not impossible but not a great situation.

It was around this time that Jim Valvano got real sick with his brain cancer and he eventually died a couple weeks later. I thought about him from time to time, and it really made me feel bad. He had recruited me for North Carolina State and I remember the day he came to our house. My mom gave him a soda—I think it was a Pepsi—and he put his arms up ready to talk in that emotional way of his and knocked the soda right on the floor, sent it flying. "Man," he said, "I must be nervous talking to the Shaq." I didn't choose his school but my parents loved him. A coach like that can come into your house and not say anything, just hold up a copy of his career record. Whenever I'd see him after that at banquets and stuff he'd be real nice and friendly. The basketball world will miss a guy like Jim Valvano.

On April 18, we beat the Celtics 88–79, putting us in a tie with Detroit for ninth place, still two games out of eighth. Litterial had a real good game off the bench with ten points. The NBA has been an adjustment for him. Matty Goukas isn't the kind of guy to get real close to his players—maybe no NBA coach is—and Litterial was used to playing for a coach, Hugh Durham of Georgia, who got really involved with his players. By this time, our thinking was that we could beat almost anybody we had to at home. Over the last two months of the season we only lost two games at home, to Seattle and to Charlotte in the game I was suspended. The difference next season is that we'll enter November with that attitude and we won't lose to anybody we shouldn't. I had 20 points and 21 rebounds, my sixth 20–20 game of the season. Once in a while I like to look at that boxscore and see more rebounds than points. It just looks fine, especially when you think that they only count rebounds by ones.

Two nights later we drilled the Bullets at home 105–86 while the Pacers were losing to the Hawks. That meant we were now only one game behind Indiana. I did that point-rebound thing again, getting 20 points and 25 rebounds, which was a team record. My goal is 40 rebounds someday. I don't think you'll see anyone get 50 because guys are such good shooters these days that there just aren't that many rebounds available. But 40 is possible. I also had a season-high six assists in this game and even led the fast break twice. I have the feeling fans really like to see that. You can hear this buzz start whenever a big man takes off dribbling full speed, probably because everybody believes he's going to trip over his own shoelaces and look like some circus clown. Not me, though. And not some other big men, either, like Hakeem and Alonzo. They let little men post up by the basket, right? So let us dribble the ball once in a while.

Early in the game Tom Gugliotta took it hard to the hole and I knocked him down and got called for a flagrant. After the game even Gugliotta said it wasn't a flagrant, just the kind of hard foul a guy makes when he's trying to protect the basket. I like Gugliotta's attitude. I don't know whether he'll be the next Larry Bird like they're making him out to be, but Gugliotta will be all right.

And then came the game that really hurt, a 126–98 loss to the Celtics at Boston. They're a proud team, and proud teams don't get embarrassed twice in a row. The Celtics learned their lesson when we pounded them a few days earlier and they were ready for us. That put our record at 39–41. We could still make the playoffs but we had to win both of our last two games against New Jersey and Atlanta and hope that Indiana lost twice and Detroit lost once. I never did feel real confident about it. My father taught me a long time ago that if you need help, you probably won't get it.

The pressure was on, but I had a good time at the game in Jersey. The day before the game I went back to the 'hood and met my Uncle Mike, who's a cop, a real tough dude. We went back to his house, and Aunt Vivian, my mom's sister, cooked us fried chicken and macaroni and cheese. If you're around when I order my last meal on earth, you can be pretty sure it'll be fried chicken and macaroni and cheese, as long as I don't have to cook it.

After that we went to a comedy club called The Peppermint Lounge—me, Uncle Mike, and four other cops. Big, black cops. Bodyguardish cops. Rough cops. Men. They were the kind of cops that, when they walk through the 'hood, you hear the bad guys saying, "Chill, man, that's Mike. That's Jerome. That's Mario." I like cops. I like being with cops. Cuts down on autograph requests. So we're chillin' in this club and my cellular phone rings and its D. Scott telling me, "I'm across the tunnel in New York at Kenny Anderson's and Derrick Coleman's party. Ride over." This is like 10:30. So the five cops and I go tearing through the Lincoln Tunnel in about five minutes and arrive at this party in a club on Broadway, all kinds of rap stars, all kinds of basketball stars. It was great. I got back about three A.M. but since I wasn't drinking or anything I didn't feel that tired.

And judging from what happened to the basket that night at the Meadowlands, I wasn't playing tired either.

Dwayne Schintzius was in the game for the Nets at the time it happened. I was glad about that. He was a Florida guy, a center from the Southeast Conference who had a reputation for being a little off the wall. Or a lot off the wall. About a minute before the basket came down I shot an airball, a jump shot, that just went right over the rim. And he ran down the court hollering, "He's scared of me, the rookie's scared of me." I told you how much I think of that word "rookie" when it's used in a negative way. And I said to him, "Schintzius, the next time I touch the ball I'm gonna dunk on your ass."

So Anthony Bowie comes down, penetrates, gives me the ball, and I took one bounce and power-dunked. It was a quick dunk, but I was going to pull myself up and yell, just to let Dwayne know I was there. But as I pulled myself up, I heard something go "clink" and I got down quick. Then the whole thing came crashing down, rim, backboard, and, finally, the shot clock at the last minute, just for dramatic effect. I could've been killed.

Believe it or not, that wasn't the closest I came to getting hurt on one of those dunks. That happened last summer when Ahmad Rashad was filming a piece for "Inside Stuff" in Los Angeles. When I dunked, I fell on my butt, and a big piece of glass was swinging and I was just staring up at it. After I got up, that one piece came down, then the whole thing came down after it. I don't want to think what would've happened if that glass had come down right away.

Filet of Shaq maybe.

But all in all, this dunk in Jersey was the best ever. The Ahmad dunk was second. And then probably comes one I did in the Sports Festival in Minneapolis when I played for the South team in the summer of 1990. I came down on a fast break, dunked real quick, and the rim came down. No backboard, just rim. I was playing against Eric Montross, the big center from North Carolina, at the time and he just threw up his arms and ducked out of the way. Coach Brown said he saw a bolt shoot right out of the backboard, like a bullet. The dunk in Phoenix that brought the whole standard down, really, was nothing compared to these, nothing. I had a better one sort of like that in my last year in college against the Australian national team. I went baseline and, when I dunked, I ripped out a chain that was anchoring the basketball support to the floor. They couldn't find another chain, and they asked me to stop dunking so hard the rest of the game. "Sorry," I told Coach Brown, "I can't play that way." I think he kept me on the bench a little longer than he had to.

Actually, I was probably fourteen or fifteen when I tore down my first basket. I couldn't even dunk on a regulation basket but this one was about nine feet. They had just built this new park with rubber courts and fiberglass boards and, when I dunked, the whole thing just came off. No videotape on that one unfortunately.

After the dunk in Jersey, Maurice Cheeks came over and said, just fooling around, "Cut that out, boy. Stop that." We went to the locker room for a forty-minute break after that and when we came back Nick really went off on them with fifty points and we won 119–116. I think the refs were mad at me for delaying the game that long. I really do. I didn't get a call the rest of the night.

What can I say? There are a lot of strong dunkers in this league, and when you just dunk on something for a long time, there's a lot of wear and tear. Basically, it's being in the right place at the right time. (Or the wrong place at the wrong time for people who don't like delays.) Sure, strength and leverage and jumping ability have a lot to do with it, but so does luck. Earlier in the season Chris Morris of the Nets brought one down in a game against the Bulls. (Maybe it's just something about the Meadowlands baskets.) He's an Auburn dude, a real athletic player but not a real strong, physical dunker. No way a skinny dude like Chris can get one on strength alone. That basket was just ready to come down. Sorry, Chris.

Naturally, there were people talking about the league having to do something about it, but I think the NBA likes it. It draws attention and headlines. They can call a technical on you for hanging on the rim, but, if someone is under you, you can hang on to protect yourself. I hung because I thought Schintzius was under me. And a lot of times when you're up there you can't decide real quick whether or not a guy's right under you so naturally you hang. You come down on somebody and it could end your career.

I don't go into a game thinking about tearing down a basket. But sometimes it happens. And if the league doesn't want it to happen, then the only answer is to get stronger rims because I'm not going to change my game.

Funny, but before the game Brian Hill, our assistant coach, said he thought something was wrong with the basket. I don't know about that, but there was something very wrong with it shortly after that.

Well, after the win over the Nets, we came back home to play Atlanta the next night. Final game of the season. We had to beat the Hawks and hope that the Heat, our old state rivals, beat Indiana. We took care of business, beating the Hawks 104–85 in a real solid game by everybody. As I said, we didn't think anybody could beat us at home by the end of the year. I closed out with 31 points and 18 rebounds.

After the game, it was kind of strange. All the fans were real happy and we were glad we had taken care of business, but there was kind of an unfinished atmosphere about the whole thing. I gave my jersey to a young boy named Alec Rollins in a fan appreciation thing. At halftime I had been presented with the Fans' Choice Award, which was given to the most popular Magic player. That meant something. Thank you, Orlando.

When we got back to the locker room, Dennis and I went into the film room to watch the remainder of the Miami-Indiana game. I didn't feel like facing all the reporters who, if the Heat had won, would be ready to ask us how we stacked up against the Knicks. New York had won the East and I would've looked forward to playing them. I also spent a few minutes chatting with Jim Kelly, the Bills' quarterback who gave me his jersey. The Heat was ahead in the first half but the Pacers rallied to win and that was it for us. Actually, Indiana and us both finished with 41–41 records and they had to go all the way to the fourth tiebreaker to decide it for them. It turned out that they had scored five more points than us in our four head-to-head matchups, which were even 2–2.

A lot of people had problems with deciding a playoff race like that, but that's the way it goes. If we had taken care of business better, we wouldn't have been put in that position. Anyway, a few weeks later, a lot of people were also complaining about the way the NBA ran the draft lottery.

The Orlando Magic were not among the complainers.

CHAPTER THIRTEEN

Going Hollywood

A few days after the regular season ended, I took off in my car. Driving always relaxes me. I told you I made the decision to leave LSU during a drive from Baton Rouge to San Antonio. And the way I got away from it all during the season was to jump in my car, turn the music up real, real loud and just drive around for a couple hours.

My destination after the season was Louisiana, but I stopped for a party in Tallahassee, Florida, stopped for a party in Mobile, Alabama, stopped for a party in New Orleans. I've got so many friends in that part of the country that I could've spent all summer going to parties.

But then I wouldn't be a serious person, right?

One special place I visited was Cecilia, Louisiana, a small

town about thirty minutes from Baton Rouge, to see a former LSU teammate named Harold Boudreaux. Well, it was sort of to see Harold. When I was in college Harold introduced me to this beautiful Creole girl named Catice Broussard. Black skin, gray eyes. Every time I came to visit Catice, her father would never let me stay at the house. So I used to stay with this woman named Pooney, an older lady who took care of Harold and his brother. So, it was just like college again. I stopped in to see Catice, then stayed with Pooney.

I was in Louisiana for a week or so, drove around, saw a lot of old friends, and started back to Orlando. Along the way I did a lot of thinking about the season, where the team had come from, where we were going, where I had come from, and where I was going.

First off, the Magic is a lot stronger franchise now than it was before I came, and I think I had something to do with that. By the end of last season we were the second biggest draw on the road behind the Bulls. Suddenly, Magic T-shirts and hats were really hot items around the league. I remember the people at the Magic gift shop had a hard time keeping Shaq merchandise in the stores, and that just means more people buying Dennis Scott stuff and Nick Anderson stuff and Scott Skiles stuff. Phone calls and mail to the Magic office quadrupled, and they had to hire a lot of extra people to handle everything. That's okay. It helps the unemployment situation in the United States. Alex Martins always says I quadrupled his workload. Sorry for that, bro—it'll make you a better person.

On the court, we finished as the most improved team in the NBA. We won 21 games the year before I came and 41 in 1992–1993 for a 20-game improvement. Next best were the Hornets and the Rockets who won 13 more. We broke the franchise record for home wins in a season with 25. We broke a few negative streaks, too. For the first time the Magic beat the Pistons, for the first time we won at Boston Garden, at the Forum in L.A. and at Portland. It's funny, but there are still four arenas where the Magic hasn't won—in Detroit, in Houston, in Miami, and in Milwaukee. We're coming in there strong next year, people, so you better be ready.

Shortly after I got back, I was named rookie of the year and accepted the award on TNT. I felt proud and happy. That put me into some pretty good company, guys like Bird and Jordan. And I felt I deserved it. Some people were saying that by the end of the year Alonzo Mourning had had a better year than me, and they're entitled to their opinion. But Alonzo got a chance to play in the playoffs and that gave everyone a few extra days to look at him. That's cool. That's gonna be me next year. But during the season I outscored Alonzo, outrebounded him, out shot-blocked him, and had a better shooting percentage. I'll tell you one team stat I'm really proud of—we held our opponents to .456 shooting, the second-lowest percentage in the league behind the Knicks. I have to think a lot of teams were thinking about me when they took it inside.

When I came in, I saw right away I could hang with the best of them. I had plusses and minuses against all the great centers, Hakeem, David, and Patrick. And I learned that, in one way, it's not any different from college. I'm still facing double-teams all the time. The difference is that they can't put a guy right in front of me from the beginning or it's an illegal defense. I'm not saying I'm the only rookie in history who got double- and triple-teamed right away, but I bet I'm one of the few. It was a learning process dealing with that, and I'm still going to be learning next year and the year after. But when I get it, look out.

But I have to get better as a player, I know that. Did somebody mention free throws? Yeah, of course they did. That's about all I heard the whole year. I made about 60 percent of my free throws, .592 to be exact. Most of the other top rookies were in the 70 percents, although Tom Gugliotta, who's a real good outside shooter, only made 64 percent. Christian Laettner made 83 percent, but shooting's his life. I'm not going to make any predictions, but all I'll say is that I'll be better. I'm not going to come back as a 93 percent foul shooter just like

Mark Price isn't going to come back as a dunker-rebounder-shot-blocker. It's not in his nature. But I'll be better. Mainly, it's so I can be the go-to guy at the end of the game, just like I am at the beginning. One disappointing thing about the NBA—and I've already talked about this—is how everyone just fouls and fouls instead of playing defense. Okay, I've got to accept that it's going to happen, even if I don't like it. So I gotta make them stop fouling me by getting better at the line.

Free throws are nothing but mechanics. It's like a car—if the fan belt runs smoothly, the car is all right, but if the fan belt has a little cut in it, the car won't quite run smoothly. During the season there was a little cut in my fan belt. And from day to day it was different. Sometimes I shot down, sometimes I kept my elbow up, sometimes I didn't follow through, sometimes the concentration wasn't there. I know I don't want to start doing crazy stuff like they tried for Wilt Chamberlain, running up to the line, standing off to the side, shooting underhand between the legs. One year when I was in college, Dale Brown tried to get me to bank my free throws, and I didn't like that idea either.

The Magic filmed me during the season and had their shooting coach, Buzzy Braman, working with me. But they didn't make a lot of changes then, and I think that was a good idea. It was better to just let me think about it, work on it myself, and get my confidence. You can change some mechanics, but there's not a lot of mystery to shooting. And whatever mystery there is, I'm going to solve.

I heard a lot about how I had to get a "pet shot," too, but I remember what Brendan Suhr said about that: "A dunk is a pretty good pet shot." Right on, Brendan. But my jump shot will get better. I had a nice stroke in high school, but I'll admit it needs some work now. I never wanted to shoot many jumpers in college and in my first year with the Magic because I thought it left me too far from the basket. Everyone was always talking about Wilt Chamberlain's fallaway jumper, but the key word for me is "fallaway," not "jumper." If a guy's going to hit a fallaway 80 percent of the time, then that's a good percentage shot. But if he's only going to hit 50 percent of the time, then that's 50 percent of the time he's not in position for an offensive rebound. I don't think that's what my team wants from me.

Everybody was always talking "sky hook" to me, but I've got to admit that I just don't like the way it looks. Kareem scored 30,000 points with it, so that means I have to shoot it, too? I don't buy that. It looks old-fashioned, it looks like it came from another generation. I'm a new-breed center, smooth, silky. I know how to shoot it but I don't *want* to shoot it, so let's end the talk about it. I'd rather make my jump-hook effective, and that's the one I'm going to get down.

Obviously, a lot changed for the Magic when Pat Williams brought out his rabbit's foot and again got the number one pick in the lottery in May even though our chances were only 1-in-66. Before then, nobody was paying too much attention to the draft because, according to the odds, we'd be picking like tenth or eleventh. On the day of the lottery I was eating over at a friend's house in Orlando when the show came on. I was only half listening until they kept announcing teams and Pat Williams was still standing there smiling. I almost dropped my food on the floor when we got the first pick. The only player we had brought in to interview was Bobby Hurley, the point guard from Duke, and I worked out with him a little bit. He would've been a good pick and he later went seventh in the draft, to Sacramento.

But when you've got number one, you start thinking about a different kind of player. Chris Webber from Michigan maybe, a power forward to help me out with rebounding? Shawn Bradley from Brigham Young maybe, a 7'6" guy to join me for an ebony and ivory twin tower? Jamal Mashburn from Kentucky maybe, a small forward who can shoot the three-pointer?

Nobody said much about Anfernee Hardaway, a Magic Johnson–type of point guard from Memphis State. It turned out I'd get to do my own research on him because we'd be hanging out together for a whole month before the draft. Both of us were going Hollywood.

●   ●   ●

I told you that William Friedkin, the director, was interested in having me play a role in a movie about college basketball called "Blue Chips." My only other movie experience was a small cameo role the summer before in *CB4*. CB4 was like a gangster rap group who scares everybody, but they're really not bad. They asked me to make up a line about them and I said: "Well, they're all right. You've got groups biting off rat heads and nobody's saying anything about them." It was a good line. It went okay.

But this would be something different, a major role with a lot of lines. I didn't spend much time thinking about it because we were in the middle of the season, but the movie people kept in touch with Leonard and they finally decided they wanted to come to Orlando to hear me read some lines. That definitely got me thinking, especially since Nick Nolte, a great actor who I had seen in *48 Hrs.*, *Cape Fear*, and *Down and Out in Beverly Hills*, was coming with him. He was going to star in the movie as a basketball coach named Pete Bell, a Bobby Knight–type of guy who gets caught up in the pressures of winning and stuff like that. They wanted me to rehearse with him a little bit.

Now, I've already told you I'm a person with a lot of self-confidence. But one thing I don't like is to look stupid. It doesn't seem to bother some people, but it bothers me. If I rap, I want to be a good rapper. If I do commercials, I want to be a good commercial actor. But acting beside Nick Nolte was something else again. It would be like if Nolte suddenly had to become a small forward for the Orlando Magic. I think he'd be nervous, too.

Leonard and I talked a little about the role and he wasn't crazy that I'd be appearing in a basketball movie. We both felt that, eventually, I'd maybe like to do some action roles, like Schwarzenegger. I wasn't kidding back at Planet Hollywood when I told Ah-nold I was going to be fighting him someday in "The Shaqinator." Leonard wondered whether I wasn't hurting myself by playing a basketball player, as if that was all I could do. But then we thought about it. I had a chance to do a movie with one of the top actors in the world directed by one of the best directors in the world, kind of like starting out with a championship team.

So, right before the All-Star break, William Friedkin, Nick Nolte, and Ron Shelton, the writer of the movie, came to Orlando to give me a mini–screen test. We did it at a suite in the Omni Hotel across from the arena. They picked two simple scenes, one where Nick meets me for the first time, and another where Nick's ex-wife, who's played in the movie by Mary McDonnell, the woman from *Dances with Wolves,* was tutoring me. Nick had to play the ex-wife. He was great, of course, except his voice was a little hoarse for the role.

My approach was to just play it natural and not pretend I was some kind of Shakespeare guy. That would be fake. They wanted to make sure of two things—that I didn't freeze up as soon as we started, and that I didn't stumble over the words. It didn't have to be perfect. It just couldn't be awful.

I already knew from the commercials that I had a feel for facial expressions and, most of all, not overacting and just being myself. And I must've been okay, because right after the rehearsal they told me they wanted me. After that it was left for Leonard and the movie execs to work out a deal. When it was all said and done, I don't want to tell you what my salary was because it would make too many out-of-work actors upset with me. But I guess they thought I brought something to it—seven-feet of something—that no one else could bring.

So right around June 1, Dennis Tracey, my cousin Brian, and I left for L.A. for a month of filming. Shezam came along, too, and pretty soon he was the best-known dog at the Four Seasons Hotel in Beverly Hills. I had my black 'Benz shipped out for $1,400. You can't style in Beverly Hills and Hollywood unless you got your own wheels and your own tunes. They got Dennis a role in the movie as a member of my team, just like at LSU.

We got a suite of rooms on the fifteenth floor, Dennis in one bedroom, me in the other, and Brian and Shezam in the middle room, which was kind of like a combination conference-meeting-living room. It's a good thing we had somebody cleaning up for us every day.

Before we started filming, Bill Friedkin invited Dennis and me to his house to discuss the movie. It turned out that when he was first planning the movie, he didn't want to cast basketball players. He wanted nonplayers who could act. But the man who suggested me turned out to be Peter Newell, whose big-man's camp I've gone to for the last two summers. Pete is a good friend of Bill's and was going to help him as a technical adviser. Pete read the script and told him: "You know, Shaquille might be good for the role of Neon." And Bill said: "Let me think about it."

My character, Neon Boudeaux, is what they call a sleeper. The idea was that he was a Creole kid from Louisiana, never played basketball in high school, went into the service, developed late, and nobody knew about him. That's not exactly my biography, but there are similarities. I knew about Louisiana from college, I was a late bloomer, not in size but in talent, I was around army people all the time, and I was kind of a sleeper when I got to San Antonio. Nobody knew about me. Nobody figured I could be any good because I hadn't gone to the right basketball camps. I knew what it was like to have to prove myself.

There were other things about Neon that fit me, too. He's a kind of laidback character, doesn't say much, doesn't let people know what's going on inside of him. Basically, he's smarter than he looks. He didn't have to be seven feet tall, but it didn't matter that he was. The script just turned him into a center.

When they signed me up, though, Bill Friedkin said that the

whole "look" of the movie changed. They couldn't have this one big basketball player running around out there with a bunch of actors. It would've looked like when Kevin McHale played in that pickup game on *Cheers* or something wack like that. So they had to go and get at least two other blue-chip guys to be on my team and a bunch of other well-known players to be on the other teams. As I said, I like to keep people employed. They needed an Indiana farmboy type who could play, so they went and got an Indiana farm boy who can play, Matt Nover, who's one of Bobby Knight's actual players. Then they needed a kind of innocent, urban kid who's a player, so they went out and found Anfernee Hardaway, who fits the type exactly. I like our team: a strong power forward, a quarterback outside, a big Creole dude inside. We could beat a lot of people, even with Nick coaching. We're called the Western University Dolphins, and Pete Newell said he wouldn't mind starting a franchise with that group.

Later on in the summer, the Orlando Magic started thinking that way, too.

Another thing that made it easy was that Bill and Ron Shelton both liked working with real people. Bill said he used real cops when he did *The French Connection* and real priests when he did *The Exorcist*. And Ron, who directed *White Men Can't Jump* and also wrote *Bull Durham*, said he had more luck with real athletes doing athletic scenes. That just makes sense. See, athletes are used to getting coached. They may not always like it, they may not always agree with the coach, but they spend a lot of time listening. They have to do things on cue. They have to do things over and over. They have to go to certain places on the floor. And guys like Anfernee and me are also used to being in front of a camera, getting interviewed, reacting to situations. All these things tie in to acting. In fact, they tie in more than I ever hoped, especially that part about doing stuff over and over.

Leonard had two worries at the beginning. He didn't want me to be in an R-rated movie because of my image. I didn't think about it one way or the other, but that's his job to think about things like that. The people at Paramount weren't sure what the movie was going to be. There was a chance it would be an R only because of language, but, when they started thinking about it, they decided it would be silly to make a movie that kids might want to see and then not let them see it. So it's a PG-13. There's nothing in there I wouldn't let a kid see. The only nasty parts are when I dunk on somebody's head.

Also, in the first script, all the blue-chip guys take something illegal during recruiting. Leonard didn't like that, either. I knew that illegal recruiting went on even if I didn't get involved in it, and I was willing to go along with the script. But Leonard held tough. That's why I like him. And that got Bill Friedkin thinking. He decided that he didn't want his message to be that every single blue-chip athlete in America accepts stuff under the table. Bill said Leonard gave him a "wake-up call." So they changed my role around so I'm not on the take. I'm not perfect, but I'm not on the take.

A lot of things about the movie business surprised me. Like they even had rehearsals. When Bill told me the first day to report for rehearsal, I just thought he meant we were going to run through it once, and then they'd turn the cameras on and we'd get it done. After going through the Reebok shoot, I knew it wouldn't be fast, but I thought we could do a scene in a day. But it doesn't happen like that in the movies. During rehearsals, they just set everything up, run through the lines, and never turn the camera on, so everybody can be prepared the next day. Hey, who am I to argue? They been doing it that way in Hollywood for seventy years. But you know me, bro, I'd rather just get it on.

Even when the cameras are rolling, they're not rolling for long. They shoot, then they have to change the lighting around, which takes forever, and then they take some stills, then they test the lighting, then they round everybody up, then they shoot again. It's like if during a basketball game they had to take down the basket and change the height of it every time somebody scored. An average day was for Dennis and I to get up at seven, be at the studio in Hollywood by eight, and stay there until six or seven at night. And during that time we might've only shot for an hour. Even on off days we were "on call," which meant we sometimes had to go back to rehearse or reshoot a scene. I'm definitely not thinking about changing careers at this point.

But you gotta make it fun. I went out there every day with the approach that it's got to be fun. Lucky for us, there was a halfcourt basket right outside where we were filming which of course they needed for the basketball scenes. That's where you could find me, Anfernee, Matt, and Dennis Tracey a lot of the time. When you see my jump shot going down this winter and ask me where it got so good, I'll just say, "Paramount, bro, Paramount."

I like everything about Bill Friedkin. I mean, the man has an Oscar (for *The French Connection*), which is like being MVP for a season. The only problem with him is that he's a stone Celtic fan. He's a good friend of Red Auerbach's, and some years he even goes up there and works out with them in rookie camp. Most days on the set he wore something, a hat or a shirt, with Celtics on it, and my goal was to convert him to be a Magic fan. I told him there's more of a future in it.

One of the things Bill encouraged was for me and all the basketball actors to speak up if we saw something wack. So I spoke up. In this one scene I'm in an English Lit. class and I'm giving the professor a little bit of a hard time.

"How come this isn't a course in African literature?" I ask him.

"Didn't you read the guide?" he said. "It's a course in English folktales."

"Well, how come it's not a course in African folk tales?"

It goes on like that and finally he says something angry to me, and I was supposed to say, "I'll take it up with my faculty adviser." But that didn't sound right to me. So I said, "I'll take it up with my coach." And for some reason it got a big laugh, sounded funny, kind of took the edge off the scene. They left it in.

Another time in the script I'm supposed to be working on a move to my left because I'm not very good at it. (See, movies aren't always realistic.) Finally I get it down and call to Nick, "Hey, coach, did you see my move to the left?" But I felt the whole thing would be more realistic if it was a spin move I was having trouble with, and Bill let me change that, too.

The only problem I had as an actor was with my volume. I talk kind of soft, and a few times Bill had to tell me to speak up. But luckily my character's supposed to be kind of soft-spoken, so I guess I have an excuse.

Almost every day Bill looked at what they call "dailies," which are clips from that day's shooting. I didn't want any part of that. See, even when you're in a movie, you don't have any idea what the whole thing looks like when it's all together. You're just filming a piece at a time and there's so much going on that you don't even see. When it's ready to come out, which is supposed to be around the time of the 1994 Final Four, I'm gonna go buy a ticket and see it for the first time like everybody else.

Well, maybe I won't buy a ticket.

I'm leaving this book in early July, just before we left for Indiana to film most of the basketball action. The movie's going to be like no other sports movie you've ever seen because we're really going to be playing all out, without a script most of the time. Whoever wins, wins. At first Bill was just going to build a gymnasium at an airport near L.A. and get like two thousand extras to be the fans. But he knew that wouldn't look right for a big-time college basketball program. So he decided to move the whole thing to Indiana and play it before real fans.

Sure, he's going to have to edit together a certain ending for a couple of the games, but, basically, he's just going to let it fly because he thinks that'll look more realistic. The guys on the other team are going to be top college players like Hurley, Acie Earl from Iowa, Chris Mills from Arizona, and maybe even Isiah Thomas. And one of the coaches on the other team is going to be Bobby Knight, who doesn't like to lose, even in a movie. But Anfernee, Matt, and I don't like to lose either.

A lot of funny things happened on the set, but one of the best was getting to meet Ed O'Neill, the guy who plays Al Bundy on *Married With Children*. Ed has a supporting part in the movie as a newspaper reporter. We exchanged autographs and I told Al—it's hard to call him anything but Al once you've seen that show—that I wanted to be on his sitcom. He said great. I told him I already had it schemed out. I would show up at the door one day with his daughter and she'd introduce me as her new black, seven-foot boyfriend. Then I made the face that he'd make on the show, and it broke him up. He was practically on the floor laughing, saying, "Let's do it, let's do it." Look for it to happen on Fox, bro.

I didn't hang out much with Nick Nolte, and I didn't expect to. He's got the major role, and the man worked so hard that he was like mentally wrung out every time he finished. But he was great to work with. He didn't come across as one of these guys who knew every secret of life just because he's a movie star. He was a real, nice, down-to-earth guy. He studied with Bobby Knight for two months to learn how to be a coach, and you can tell he learned his lessons well. In his past, though, he was more of a football player and he didn't know every little detail about basketball. One day Bill was filming some action footage and Dennis was working real hard. He got tired eventually and he kept raising his hand, the signal basketball players use when they want to come out. But Nick just kept looking at him and later he told Dennis, "Oh, I thought you were just waving to me." Good going, Nick. Get that turkey in shape. If I ever get that role when I fight Arnold Schwarzenegger, I want to bring along Nick on my side.

I found time to work on a few other things over the summer out in L.A., too, but not a lot. Sometimes after I finished at the movie set I went into the studio to work on my rap album that's due out sometime during this season. And I also went to another studio one day to act out the moves that are going to be digitized into two video games for Electronic Arts. One is a three-on-three, street-type basketball game. There's going to be three levels—nice level, trash-talking level, and double trash-talking level. The last one will have stuff on it like, "You can't stop me, boy" and "Take that, boy." I thought about maybe having a flopping level and inviting Karl Malone and Bill Laimbeer out to pose for it, but I don't think anyone would buy it.

The other one is a martial arts–type game. The story is, somebody has kidnapped my daughter and my karate master, and I have to fight all these martial arts dudes to get them back.

That actually fit in with what I wanted to do physically this summer, to work on my legs and get more flexibility. On my off days from the movie I worked out with a guy named Trent Suzuki, who was amateur world kick-boxing champion. I want springs, I want hops out of this world, Michael Jordan–type hops, Shawn Kemp–type hops. I played a lot of pickup ball over at UCLA, but I think the most important thing I did was work on those legs.

● ● ●

On the day before the draft, June 29, the Magic moved Matty Goukas to a position upstairs and promoted Brian Hill, Matty's top assistant, to head coach. I'm not in the business of criticizing coaches. I'm in the business of respecting coaches. Right after last season was over, Nick Anderson talked to a reporter from Chicago and complained about Matty. He said Matty was too laidback and needed to relate to younger players better. He also indicated that other players on the team, especially me, agreed with him.

Now, I'll tell you what I don't like. People speaking for me and telling other people my opinions. I spent a whole season talking to the press without ever once putting my foot in my mouth or saying something I didn't mean. I was pretty proud of that. So what I didn't need was Nick speaking for me.

Matty knew his basketball. But maybe he didn't communicate it as well as he should. Maybe he didn't get everything he could out of his players. Maybe that was his players' fault, maybe it was his fault, maybe it was a little bit of both. Probably both. But he's not there and somebody else is. And I'm very happy with the somebody else.

Matty was a little bit distant from his players. That was just his style, that's all. But I got very close to Brian Hill during the year. He was the one waiting for me when I came off the floor to tell me, ''You're not doing all you can to help us win this game tonight.'' And then he'd tell me what it was, whether it was helping out on defense or not wanting the ball enough. I felt I had a real close relationship with Brian. I'm not the one to give Brian Hill any advice about basketball. He knows ball. All I'm going to say is this, Brian: come in and let everyone know who's boss. Right from the beginning. And I'm behind you.

● ● ●

The Four Seasons in Beverly Hills had twenty-four-hour room service, real friendly employees, and a couple great restaurants (I ate a lot of lean turkey), but it didn't have TNT. So I didn't hear David Stern call out the name Chris Webber just like he called out the name Shaquille O'Neal last year. And I didn't hear the trade that was announced thirty minutes later when we gave up Chris to get Anfernee, who had been picked at No. 3 by Golden State. Soon after I got about a dozen phone calls and I told everybody the same thing: I couldn't be happier.

Somehow, everybody had gotten the idea that I wanted Chris Webber for our team. I have nothing against Chris, and we did talk a couple of times. He made the comment that he hoped he was playing with the Magic because he could shoot an air ball, then act like it was a pass when I dunked it. During the season I used to kid Leonard Armato all the time that he was putting me on hold to take calls from Webber. But I never ·said Chris Webber was the only one I wanted.

The truth is, from the beginning I wanted Anfernee Hardaway.

People forget that I have a history with Anfernee. We were on the same South team that won the gold medal in the Sports Festival in Minneapolis. People forget that I saw what a great player he was then. Scott Skiles did a fine job for us at point guard, and I hope he's around to help school Anfernee. But Anfernee and I found out during the movie that we had something real special, a chemistry, and I see us as a team that can take the Magic to the next level.

And that's where I want to go. No, that's where I *have* to go. I know that. I know that all the commercials, all the movie roles, all the press stories won't mean anything unless I get a championship. It took Magic just one year. It took Michael Jordan seven years. Charles Barkley doesn't have one yet. Patrick Ewing doesn't have one yet. Lots of great players never get one. But I'm going after it. If not this next season, then the one after it, or the one after that.

The Shaq Attack ain't stopping, bro, it's just getting started.

My ball, my court, my game.

PEN